Music for Young Listeners

Series for Listeners

BY LILLIAN BALDWIN

THE GREEN BOOK
THE CRIMSON BOOK
THE BLUE BOOK

MUSIC TO REMEMBER

A LISTENER'S ANTHOLOGY
OF MUSIC
(In Two Volumes)

MUSIC FOR YOUNG LISTENERS

THE GREEN BOOK

BY *Lillian Baldwin*

Silver Burdett Company

MORRISTOWN, N. J.

CHICAGO SAN FRANCISCO DALLAS ATLANTA

Grateful acknowledgment is made to publishers
for permission to quote from copyrighted scores.
Credits are given on pages where themes appear.

SILVER BURDETT COMPANY

COPYRIGHT, 1951

△

Printed in the United States of America

Contents

THE GREEN BOOK

v

TO THE YOUNG LISTENER

This is a book for listeners. Among the many people who listen to music in these days of phonographs, radios, and concerts, there is a new and important person called the "musicianly listener." Schools are interested in his training. Books are written for him, and musicians are glad to have him at their concerts. This good listener is not a person who merely hears music, letting it go in at one ear and out at the other. He thinks about what he hears. And he is proud to know about music, even though he himself cannot sing very well or play an instrument. Singers and players should be good listeners too. So, you see, a book for listeners is everybody's book.

There are two slightly different kinds of music which every good listener is pretty sure to meet. The difference is not so much in the music as in the composer's main idea as he wrote it. Some composers are most interested in making beautiful patterns of tones which express feelings. They are rather like the artists who make the designs for wallpapers, dishes, silks and cottons, and the hundreds of pretty things we see every day. Other composers are thinking of some particular story or picture which they want their music to suggest. The difference in these two purposes has given us the two kinds of music which we shall call "Pattern Music" and "Story and Picture Music."

As you read this book you will find that the pattern music in Part I can suggest delightful stories and pictures to the listener who has a good imagination. And the story and picture music in Part II follows music's patterns, or it could not tell its story or paint its picture. Many of the pieces could belong to either part of the book. There is so much likeness in these two kinds of music that the difference is not too important. Why, then, do we tell you about it? Because it is one of the things every musicianly listener is supposed to know, so why not you?

1

Part One

PATTERN MUSIC

THE PATTERNS of music are interesting. They are also so important that young listeners should know about them. When grown people say, "Oh, children could never understand this or that," I like to reply, "But you'd be surprised how much they can understand. Maybe you don't know how bright children are!" So I'm going to tell you something about the patterns of music, particularly those of music for instruments. I shall not try to explain these patterns, but only tell you why they are important and where some of them came from, many long years ago.

A pattern, as you know, is just a plan for making or doing something. Men don't nail a lot of boards together, hoping they'll turn out to be a house. They think before they nail. They even draw the plan on paper. When the house is finished and you have moved in, the plan is still there. You have to live with it! And if the kitchen is too small or the front door is in the wrong place, the pattern is to blame.

Hundreds of plans or patterns are used every day in the world's work. Even our play has its patterns. What are the rules of baseball but patterns which the players and the watchers have to follow? Nature has wonderful patterns—always the same kind of leaf on the maple tree, yet no two exactly alike. It is not surprising then to learn that music, too, has its patterns.

There is an amusing story of Joseph Haydn, a composer whose music is famous for its clear and beautiful patterns. When he was a very little boy he wanted to write a piece of music. He found some paper and covered it with notes. "I thought it must be all right," he said, "if the paper was nice and full of notes." Imagine his disappointment when he dis-

3

covered that there was no tune on his "nice, full paper"—only a lot of meaningless notes!

Little Joseph Haydn had to find out for himself what I am telling you. It is that a page of scattered notes is no more a piece of music than a page of jumbled words is a story. Notes have to be put together in patterns that express feeling. We call this pattern-making *composing* music. There are patterns of tones and patterns of rhythms. It takes both to make a tune.

Some of music's patterns are simple, like those of folk songs in which there are, perhaps, two or three ideas or parts to the tune, with the main one cleverly repeated. Other patterns, like those used for big symphonies, have many parts and are not so easy to follow.

Music's patterns were never meant to make compositions sound alike, as if they were things turned out by a factory. Instead, the patterns help the composer to make his piece sound different from all others, without getting off the track. To suit their own fancies, composers have made so many little changes in the patterns that no two pieces of music have ever been exactly alike. Isn't this really wonderful when you think of how many thousands of pieces there are!

Another interesting thing about music's patterns is that they were not all made at one time by a few clever men who said "This is the pattern that must be used for a song; that one, for a symphony." Music's patterns grew with the enjoyment of music. If one part of a tune was particularly pleasing, then a pattern was made in which that part could be heard several times. And to keep even a good tune from growing tiresome, another plan was made to change the tune a little, every time it was repeated.

It took many years and the help of many unknown people to make the patterns of the music we enjoy. Great composers like Bach and Haydn helped the most, by improving the patterns and adding their own bright ideas. Music's patterns are old, but they are still very much alive. Like sturdy old trees, they put out fresh leaves every year, and even a new branch now and then!

We must turn to the history books to find how and where music got some of its best patterns. Music was centuries old before there were pieces written specially for instruments and for listeners. Many of the early pieces were written for the

4

organ. Quite naturally, the composers of these organ pieces imitated the wonderful singing heard in the old churches. But outside of church, most people enjoyed music only by singing and dancing to it.

There were instruments, to be sure—drums and pipes and queer little harps that strummed along with the singing and marked the rhythms for dancing feet. But the very old instruments had only a few tones, and many of them were too wheezy and scratchy to be called musical. Those who played them may have liked them. The singers and dancers were probably having too good a time to notice the wheezy, scratchy tones. But a listener would have had little pleasure in a tune played on those old instruments.

As time went on, men began to make better instruments. Early in the seventeenth century the workshops of Italy were turning out wonderful new violins. Fine keyboard instruments, called harpsichords and clavichords, the ancestors of our pianos, were taking the place of the little strumming harps. People were delighted with these new instruments. They wanted to play them and to hear them. No doubt many a singer and dancer was asked to keep still so that listeners could enjoy the beautiful smooth tones of the new violins. It wasn't long before people were asking for a new kind of music that would show off the tones of the fine new instruments. Before composers could write this new *instrumental music,* they had to have new patterns.

Song tunes were not quite the right patterns for instrumental music. They were made for human voices which can never go as high or as low as a fine instrument. It seemed a pity not to use those extra high and low instrument tones. Besides, the song patterns were too short. We like to sing the same tune several times if there are different words each time. But to play or hear the same tune over and over can be tiresome. Many of the song tunes had been written to fit certain word patterns and, when played without their words, the tunes sounded rather lost. No wonder composers thought that a piece for instruments should be more interesting than a short song tune stripped of its words and played over and over again.

The old dance tunes, of which every country had a great number, offered more promising patterns. Since they had never had any words, the dance tunes lost nothing when played for listeners. They had the sturdy rhythms of the dances for which they were made. They stepped an orderly pattern of just so many beats to the measure and so many measures to the tune. The listener as well as the dancer could follow the music and not get lost. Best of all, there were so many different dance patterns from which a composer could choose. And if he put several of these dance-pattern tunes together, he could make a set, or *suite*, of pieces long enough to show off the new instruments and please both the players and the listeners.

So you see how, keeping their dance names, the old dance tunes became the patterns for the first instrumental music. They proved to be such good patterns that composers are still using them. And no matter what musical styles may spring up, it's a pretty safe guess that listeners a hundred years from now will still be enjoying pieces called *Minuet, Gavotte,* and *Jig.*

The most important thing to remember about music patterns is that every piece has them. Even the simplest little folk tune has rhythm patterns and tone patterns. Without them it wouldn't be music.

Often, in the music of Haydn or Mozart, the patterns are so beautiful that, as we listen, we do not want to think of a story or a picture. This is pure music, "pattern music," we might say. We enjoy it in much the same way that we enjoy the shape and color of a flower or the wonder of a sunset. We *feel* the beauty. And if our feeling stirs our fancy and we think of a story or picture, that too is pleasant. But the music remains pure music—beautiful tones composed in beautiful patterns.

1.

George Frederick Handel

Halle—1685
London—1759

Many years ago, when the United States was only a group of little colonies bordering the Atlantic Ocean, a boy by the name of George Frederick Handel was born in the small German city of Halle. The people of Halle loved music so much that every evening a choir would go up into the high tower of one of the old churches and sing for all the town to hear.

The boy Handel would listen, spellbound, to the melodies that came floating down through the twilight. He was sure that music was the loveliest thing in the world! He wanted to make music himself. So he and his playmates gathered together all the whistles, drums, triangles, and noisemaking toys in the neighborhood and had a toy band. George Frederick decided that he would be a musician when he grew up.

But Dr. Handel, the boy's father, had other plans. He had decided that his son should become a lawyer. Dr. Handel didn't think much of music. He said, "Music is an occupation of little dignity and only to be used as an entertainment." Very sternly he ordered the boy to give up the silly notion of becoming a musician. As for the toy band, Dr. Handel said he wanted to hear no more of such "jingling."

George Frederick was bitterly disappointed. His kind Aunt Anna felt so sorry for him that she gave him a small keyboard instrument. They put it up in the attic where its sound would not disturb Dr. Handel. There is a story and even a painting of the little boy sitting up there in his long white nightgown, late at night, picking out the tunes he loved.

One Sunday when George Frederick was about eight years old, he went with his father to the Duke's chapel in a nearby town. He listened eagerly, as he always did, when there was music to be heard. At the close of the service the organist, who had noticed this same child watching at other rehearsals, asked him if he would like to play the organ. He lifted him to the organ bench.

George Frederick's legs were too short to reach the pedals—you know an organ is played with the feet as well as the hands —but he could manage the keys. The organist was astonished. Soon the chapel was filled with music, as the great organ responded to the touch of those small, masterly hands. The Duke, who had lingered to talk with some gentlemen, was surprised to see so small a performer at so large an instrument. He asked who the child was and sent at once for the father. Dr. Handel was annoyed. George Frederick and his music again! He told the Duke that his son was to be a lawyer. The Duke replied that it would be wicked to waste such a gift as this child had, and ordered Dr. Handel to let the boy study music.

It was a happy little Handel who went to work with the best music teachers in Halle. He soon learned all that they could teach him. He also kept up his other studies and, to please his father, entered the University of Halle. By the time he was sixteen, George Frederick was playing the organ in the cathedral and directing the choir. He was even composing much of the church music, which was one of the duties of a German organist in those days.

Young Handel soon wanted more music than he could get in Halle. He had heard of that wonderful new kind of stage play called *opera,* in which the actors sing their parts instead of speaking them. He had to know all about it! So, in his eighteenth year, he said good-by to Halle and set out for the north German city of Hamburg, where opera was flourishing. He earned his living in Hamburg by teaching and playing the violin in the opera orchestra. In his free time he was learning to write operas. This he did so well that two of his operas were performed.

But all the while Handel was dreaming of Italy, for Italy was the birthplace of opera and, at that time, the center of the musical world. He put every spare penny into an Italian study fund, which grew until, at the end of three years, he was able to leave Hamburg and go to Italy.

Handel went to Florence, Rome, Naples, and Venice. He visited opera houses, palace concert rooms, and beautiful old churches ringing with glorious music. It was indeed a dream come true! He met many of the famous musicians of the day. It was wonderful to hear their music and their talk about music and life. Handel worked hard and became well known as a harpsichord player and a brilliant young composer.

After three years Handel went back to Germany, this time to the city of Hanover. He was given a fine position as court musician. Again he grew restless. London was now the city of his dreams, for he had heard great tales of what they were doing with Italian opera in London. The story of Handel's London adventures is long and interesting. Those adventures lasted more than forty years! Handel became an English citizen and was known as Mr. Handel of London.

Handel wrote music to be sung, and music for all kinds of instruments. He wrote concert music, church music, and operas. His finest works are his oratorios. An *oratorio* is a story set to music and sung by soloists and choruses, with an orchestra playing the accompaniment. It is somewhat like an opera except that it has no acting, no stage pictures and no special costumes for the singers. Handel's most famous oratorio tells the Bible story of Christ's life. It is called *Messiah*. Although it was written more than two hundred years ago, every year, at Christmas time, people all over the world listen to the *Messiah* and love it. Handel, the man who wrote that wonderful music, will always be remembered. And some of us like to remember the little boy, George Frederick, who listened to the tunes from the tower in old Halle—a little boy who loved music and gave his life to it.

WATER MUSIC

Young George Frederick Handel spent three happy years studying and writing music in Italy. It was there that his early operas were performed before cheering audiences. Many travelers from all over Europe came to enjoy Italian sunshine and music. Among them was a German prince, the Elector of Hanover, Handel's home state. This prince was so proud and pleased with his young countryman's music that he invited Handel to come to the court of Hanover. He made him Master of the Royal Chapel and director of court music. This was a great honor for a young musician.

But Handel was restless. Compared with the gay Italian

9

cities, Hanover seemed a dull and sleepy little place. He wanted to go to London where the musical life was said to be quite exciting. So he asked the Prince to let him visit England. The Prince agreed, but made Handel promise to come back to Hanover within a reasonable length of time.

Handel had a wonderful time in London. The English people were delighted with his operas. The Queen of England praised his harpsichord and organ playing. He composed a fine piece in honor of her birthday and wrote special music for victory celebrations of the English army. He was given a royal pension by the Queen. Meanwhile, the "reasonable length of time" had lengthened into years. Handel's prince in Hanover was highly displeased with his court musician because he did not return as he had promised he would.

Then the Queen of England died and a strange thing happened. When they began looking about among the royal aunts, uncles, and cousins to find who should be the next ruler of England, they chose the son of an English princess who had married a German prince. This man was none other than the Elector of Hanover, who now became King George I of England! An angry prince in faraway Hanover was bad enough. But to have him suddenly come to London, as the new king, put Handel in a very bad spot.

There are several stories about how this affair was patched up. One of them says that Handel waited in his London house hoping to be invited to take part in the coronation celebration. No invitation came. Here was Handel, the pet of musical London, the composer who had been writing music for all the court ceremonies, sitting at home unnoticed and completely out of luck!

As Handel was wondering what to do, he learned, so this story goes, that there was to be a great festival and parade in honor of the King's birthday. The streets of old London were so rough and so narrow that this festival was to be held on the river Thames, which flows right through the city. Handel had an idea.

On the evening of the royal birthday, the river was alive with gaily decorated boats. In a gorgeous, brightly lighted barge rode the King and his courtiers, a grand sight for the people watching from the river banks. Just behind the King's barge came another on which sat fifty musicians led by an

10

anxious composer. They began to play some new and beautiful music. The King was delighted with this pretty compliment. And when he was told that this music had been written by George Frederick Handel, his anger disappeared, as bad feeling often does at the sound of beautiful music. King George not only forgave Handel for staying away from Hanover, but also appointed him musician at his court in London. This time Handel was quite willing to stay at his post.

Some scholars say that Handel had already been forgiven by his prince, who ordered him to write this music. Whatever may be the exact story, the music and the picture of the water festival are just the same. And, best of all, that music sounds as charming today as when it floated over the river Thames, more than two hundred years ago.

Bourrée

Handel's *Water Music* is a set of short pieces made up of an introduction, a song tune, and several dance tunes. Handel was very fond of the old dance patterns and often used them for his own tunes.

The *bourrée* is a dance of the French woodcutters, from whom it takes its name. There is a suggestion of wooden shoes, as the dancers click their heels together on the first beat of every measure and stamp on the third beat. The bourrée leaps and skips and goes so fast that the players have to play twice as fast as usual to keep up.

The *Water Music* bourrée has two little tunes. First:

Violin I *pp* *leggiero*

and then:

staccato
Violin I

Although these tunes sound different, they have a teasing likeness. Some of their measures are exactly alike. Together they make a gay and lively dance that is over almost before we have a chance to hear it. This is a good pattern for gay music.

11

Hornpipe

The *hornpipe* is an old English dance. Historians say that it gets its name from a queer old instrument with a bell-shaped end made of horn, which was used to play for dancing. The dance called hornpipe is a solo dance. Because it was danced without a partner, and needed so little space that it could be done on the deck of a small ship, the hornpipe became a favorite dance among British sailors. It was clever of Handel to choose a sailor's dance for his *Water Music,* and a British sailor's dance at that!

As we listen to this music we can picture a group of jolly sailor boys having some fun on deck. "Hi, Jack, give us a dance!" they cry. Jack Tar (the oboe) steps out into the circle. While the others clap and slap their knees, Jack does this lively step:

"Ho, I can do that too!" says Piccolo Peter, and up he jumps and does the very same step.

"Try this one!" shouts Jack and leads off in a different step:

Again Peter follows him and not only does the second step, but adds a little fancy business of his own at the end.

This music sounds old-fashioned to us. It is sweet and thin like much of the music written for the orchestras of long ago. The orchestra was small in Handel's time. Many of the instruments we know today had not yet been invented.

Because both of these dances are so short, our orchestras usually play the bourrée over again after the hornpipe— making a sort of hornpipe sandwich! But a good listener can always tell where one tune ends and the other begins. It helps if you learn to whistle the first theme of each of the dances. Many of Handel's tunes are good for whistling.

Largo—XERXES

Handel's *Largo* is often played by church organists. You may even hear the choir singing it, for someone has put church words to this tune. And you will most certainly hear this piece at some concert or on the radio, for it is one of Handel's most beautiful and best-known tunes. *Largo* is an Italian word meaning slow and stately, which is exactly the way this music sounds.

People everywhere know and love Handel's *Largo,* but very few of them know that it was written as part of his opera *Xerxes.* In the opera, the hero comes out into a garden where a great tree is growing. Its broad, leafy branches make a pool of shade on the grass. The tree is strong and beautiful. As the hero looks at the tree he thinks, "It is like a friend! I hope no storm will ever harm it!" Then he puts these thoughts into song:

Thy soft leafy branches,
O beautiful tree,
Like the arms of a friend
Seem to reach out to me.
May thunder and lightning
Ne'er bring thee to harm,
Nor thy quiet be broken
By wild wind and storm.
Oh, no other tree
Casts a shadow so fair,
Or with such sweet fragrance
Perfumes the night air. [L.L.B.]

(The opera "Xerxes" was written and sung in Italian. The English words give you the thought of this song to a tree, but they do not fit the tune.)

This is the tune of *Largo,* Handel's song to a tree:

Think about this tune, after you hear all of it. Does it seem the right kind of music for a beautiful, big tree? Do you know a tree for which this music would be suitable?

Many poets and composers have written in praise of trees. There is a lovely old Christmas carol about the fir tree—*O Tannenbaum.* Schubert wrote a fine song about a linden tree.

13

There are many poems about trees. Here is the first stanza of a poem by Edwin Markham, called "A Song to a Tree":

> Give me the dance of your boughs, O tree,
>   Whenever the wild wind blows;
> And when the wind is gone, give me
>   Your beautiful repose.

There is another poem, called "Good Company," by Karle Wilson Baker, which begins:

> Today I have grown taller from walking with the trees.
> The seven sister poplars that go softly in a line.

It is easy to understand why poets write about trees as if they were friends! It is also easy to understand why people have made church music of Handel's *Largo*. After all, the hero of this old opera was praising God when he praised the splendid tree. Love of any beautiful thing gives us much the same feeling we have in church. We call that feeling "reverence."

FIREWORKS MUSIC

Composers of long ago did not often give their pieces story titles, such as *The Dancing Doll,* or *Dreaming,* or *The Music Box.* Dance names, like minuet or gavotte, were used for pieces composed in dance patterns. And if the music was song-like, it was often called *Air.* Many pieces had only their tempo or speed signs for titles. A lively piece was called *Allegro,* which is the Italian word for lively. A slow and dignified piece, like Handel's song to a tree, might be called simply *Largo,* which means slow.

Fireworks Music certainly sounds like a story title. If a modern composer had written it, we might expect all kinds of whizz-banging! Remembering Handel and the fashion of his day, we do not expect to find fireworks in the music itself. However, there were fireworks a-plenty in the story from which this music takes its name!

In the year 1749—more than two hundred years ago—a long and foolish European war was just ending. Everyone is always glad when a war is over. Although the English people had not been mixed up in this particular war, they wanted to celebrate the peace. Their king, George II, loved a celebration.

14

His people were always glad of a holiday, so great preparations were made. In the Green Park in London they built a flimsy, wooden building, made to look like a Greek temple. On top of it were figures of Neptune, the sea god, and Mars, the war god, and even a figure of King George, himself, handing out peace to a fat lady representing England.

On all special occasions, whether it was the Queen's funeral or the return of a victorious general, there had to be special music. The King would shout, "Send for Mr. Handel!" and Mr. Handel would be ordered to compose something new and suitable. This time it was to be very special music. They had built a musicians' gallery and brought cannon which were to thunder the royal salute and also let off a grand bang in the loud places in the music!

But the most important part of this celebration was to be the fireworks. There was a huge sun on a pole and there were all sorts of fancy shapes and figures—such fireworks as London had never dreamed of!

From an old magazine comes the report that, after a grand opening piece, "composed by Mr. Handel," a signal was given for the fireworks, which began with a royal salute of 101 cannon and many other big guns. But the fireworks were a fizzle. Those fine figures which were to have shone in glowing colors wouldn't work. "Men climbed like monkeys with torches and lit them again and again." Then, to everybody's horror, the Greek temple was set on fire. In a few minutes the Green Park was a mass of roaring flames. Crowds of shouting, terrified people fought their way toward the gates. It was, indeed, such fireworks as London had never dreamed of!

The next morning nothing was left of this elaborate show but Handel's music—an opening piece and five short tunes which were to have illustrated some of the special fireworks! No wonder they called it *Fireworks Music!*

This music had the nicest kind of a performance later that spring. It was played to raise money for the Foundling Hospital in London. "Foundling" is an old-fashioned name for a child who has no home or parents. Handel had never married and, although he had a house and servants, he really had no home, and, of course, no children. He was invited to the finest houses in London and praised by kings and princes, but he was a lonely man. One of his greatest pleasures, as he grew

15

older, was giving concerts and raising money for the homeless, fatherless children in the Foundling Hospital. He loved to think of these little waifs growing fat and rosy on soup and milk his money had bought, and dancing for joy at the Christmas treat sent by Mr. Handel! So, you see, *Fireworks Music* has a bright and pretty story after all.

Allegro

And now the music—the five short tunes which were to have illustrated the special fireworks, called "set pieces." We first hear a little piece called *Allegro,* which starts out:

con brio

and goes cheerily on its way. Someone gave this *Allegro* another name, *La Rejouissance,* which means "The Rejoicing."

There is a second part, in which the tune seems to question:

and answer:

and then come to a very decided ending:

Perhaps this was one of the places where they intended to fire off the cannon!

Alla Siciliana

The second piece is marked *Alla Siciliana,* which means "like a dainty Sicilian shepherd's dance." It is also sometimes called *La Paix*—"The Peace." Peaceful indeed is the quiet

16

melody:

with the violins singing so sweetly together.

Bourrée

Again, as in the *Water Music,* Handel chose the old French woodcutter's dance, the bourrée, as the pattern for the liveliest part of his *Fireworks Music.*

The Fireworks bourrée steps off gaily:

and keeps its lively motion going until the very end.

Minuet I

The minuet, "the dance of the little steps," was a great favorite in Handel's time. People liked to dance it, and composers liked to use it as a pattern for their music. Handel wrote two minuets for his *Fireworks Music.*

The first minuet is very short and very dainty. First this little tune:

followed by another which climbs up:

then sinks back with a graceful bow.

17

Minuet II

The second minuet is much more sturdy than the first:

You can feel the drum beats in this music. Handel loved the drums and even when he wrote dainty music for the strings to play, he made the cellos and basses sound like drums!

Like so many of the old-fashioned tunes, this minuet has a second part:

which is repeated loudly to make a pompous ending for the royal *Fireworks Music*.

2.

Wolfgang Amadeus Mozart

Salzburg—1756
Vienna—1791

The Mozart story begins almost two hundred years ago, in the Austrian city of Salzburg. It begins in a happy home. Leopold Mozart, the father, was an earnest, hard-working man. His father had owned a little book-binding shop, but the son, Leopold, had not been content to spend his life sewing and gluing books. He wanted to be a musician. So he studied and worked away at music until he became a very good violinist and a fairly good composer. Leopold Mozart wrote the first instruction book for violin playing ever published. When he was made director of the Archbishop of Salzburg's orchestra, everybody thought him a very successful young man.

The Mozarts lived in a comfortable old house which is now the famous Mozart Museum. Their living room was a cheerful place with its big tile stove and its windows gay with flowers. Here Mr. Canary trilled in his cage. Here Leopold Mozart and his friends spent many hours talking about music, and playing their trios and quartets. Leopold's wife, pretty, laughing Anna Maria, was happy all the day long, keeping her shining house, cooking good food, and looking after her dear, doll-like children.

There were two children—Marianne, whose pet name was Nannerl, and little Wolfgang. Wolfgang had a pretty middle name. It was Amadeus, which means "loved of God." That name seems to suit this little boy to whom God gave so much —a happy home, a merry disposition, and the most beautiful gift of all, music.

Nannerl was five years older than Wolfgang. When she was eight her father began giving her lessons on the clavier—an old-fashioned instrument that looks like a tiny piano. Nannerl's music lessons interested three-year-old Wolfgang. He

19

wanted to play, too. They would find him perched at the clavier, exploring the keyboard with his tiny fingers. How pleased he was when he discovered the nice sound you can make by striking *thirds*—that is, two white piano keys, separated by just one white key. Soon he began to pick out the tunes of Nannerl's little pieces.

Leopold Mozart was amused and, half in fun, gave Wolfgang a few lessons. Soon his amusement turned to amazement at the way this baby could learn. He just went romping through his sister's pieces. One of Nannerl's old music books may still be seen in the Mozart museum at Salzburg. On the margins of its pages the father wrote such notes as this: "This minuet and trio were learned by Wolfgang in half an hour, at half past nine at night, on January 26th, 1791, one day before his fifth birthday."

Wolfgang was not satisfied with playing other people's music. He began to write little minuets and pieces of his own. An old letter tells this story of the small composer. One evening the father brought a friend home with him. The men found four-year-old Wolfgang busy with pen and paper. They asked him what he was doing and he answered, "Writing a concerto for the clavier." A *concerto* is a very elaborate piece for a solo instrument and orchestra. The men were surprised that the child even knew the word and they asked to see his wonderful concerto. What they saw seemed to be just a daub of notes mixed with blots for, says the letter, "The little fellow had dipped his pen every time down to the very bottom of the ink bottle, so that as soon as it reached the paper, down fell a blot. But that did not disturb him in the least. He rubbed the palm of his hand over it, wiped it off, and went on with his writing."

The men laughed, but as they looked closer they saw that this inky mess really was music after all. "But," cried the father, "No one on earth could play it, it is so difficult!"

"Yes," said Wolfgang, "That is why it is a concerto. It must be practiced until it is perfect. Look, this is how it goes." And he hopped to the clavier and showed them!

The two men were thrilled, as people always are by a wonder-child. It is like magic to see a child do what grown men have worked years and years to learn to do. Wolfgang was a wonder, there was no doubt about it. Nannerl, too, was a remarkable player. As Leopold Mozart thought about his gifted children, an idea came to him. Why not show them to the world? In those days there were no public concerts given in halls, to which people paid admission. The concerts were given in the palaces and houses of rich noblemen. But these dukes and counts and princes were the very ones who made it possible for musicians to earn a living. If only they could be interested in the children, the Mozart family fortune would be made!

So when Wolfgang was six years old and Nannerl eleven, the Mozart family started out. At first they went to nearby courts. The children did so well that their ambitious father then planned a long tour. They would go to Paris, stopping at all the large cities on the way, and then across the channel to faraway London. It was all so new and strange to the small travelers! Nannerl kept a diary and when she first saw the ocean she wrote, "How the sea runs away and comes back again!"

Everywhere they went the little Mozarts astonished people. Nannerl played the clavier and the harpsichord—another old keyboard instrument—with all the skill of a grown-up artist. Wolfgang played the clavier, the violin, and, before long, the organ, too. People were surprised by his playing, and even more surprised by his wonderful memory and his understanding of music. The best musicians of the different cities delighted in testing him. They would play quite difficult pieces, then the little boy would repeat them, playing by ear. Or they would give him a scrap of a tune—a theme—and he would make it into a complete piece, playing it right off. Music seemed to come to him out of the air! And, most wonderful of all, this child would sit down at a desk and write music— even pieces for orchestra with parts for the many instruments —as easily as you would write a letter.

People enjoyed seeing the children as well as hearing them. They must have made a pretty picture. Nannerl had a little white satin court dress, and apple-cheeked Wolfgang wore a powdered wig, a coat of lilac velvet, and a tiny sword at his side. They were dear little people, always polite but quite childish. Wolfgang would scramble up on the lap of an empress or romp with little princesses as naturally as if they had been his Salzburg neighbors. Once he slipped and fell on the palace floor in Vienna. Little Princess Marie Antoinette, who later became Queen of France, ran to help him. "You are nice," he said, "and I will marry you." And once, when the Emperor, himself, was playing, Wolfgang, to his father's dismay, called out, "Good!" and later, "Oh, that was wrong!" He was a simple, merry-hearted child, and being a wonder-boy did not spoil his fun.

But when Wolfgang began to play, he would grow strangely serious. Then he became a little prince, a very haughty one. Sometimes he would refuse to play until he was sure that his listeners loved music and knew something about it.

Nannerl and Wolfgang were showered with presents by their royal admirers. They had enough medals, enough jewelry and costly trinkets to have opened a shop! And they were petted and praised until they would certainly have been quite spoiled if their parents had not been sensible. Their father kept them at their studies and their practicing even when they were traveling. "My children are used to hard work," he said. He also kept them at their prayers. They were taught to think of God's goodness to them rather than of their own smartness. No matter how busy or tired they were, or how strange the place in which they happened to be, God was not forgotten.

After a long stay in London the Mozarts went to Holland, then back to Paris, and finally home to Salzburg. They had been away for more than three years!

Fine as it was to be seeing the world and winning the praise of kings and queens, there was another side to these wonderful journeys. They were not made in a few hours in comfortable Pullman cars, steamships, automobiles, or airplanes. Going to England meant pitching and tossing in nasty little boats that turned a traveler's stomach wrongside out. Traveling across country in Mozart's time meant days and weeks of jolting over rough and muddy roads in chilly coaches. How dreary it was when a horse went lame or the coach broke down!

Once the Mozarts had to wait a whole day in a little town while a wheel was being mended. Father Mozart was not the man to waste any day. He took seven-year-old Wolfgang to the village church and showed him how the organ worked. Before they left, the boy was pedaling away at a great rate. This was the beginning of Mozart's organ playing.

Frau Mozart must often have been anxious about the children's food. One day they might have to eat some soggy mess at a little wayside inn, and the next day they would be stuffed with sweets by the hand of a princess. No more attention was paid to bedtime than if the children had been little pet animals.

Worst of all was the excitement and strain of showing off. It was particularly hard on Wolfgang, for people were always trying him out. They would think up silly stunts like covering the keyboard with a cloth or asking him to play with one finger. An archbishop did not believe the wonderful tales about Wolfgang. He had the child shut up in a room by himself, for a week, to see if he could compose an oratorio. Wolfgang did it, but it makes one angry to think that people could treat a little boy so!

It is no wonder that the poor little Mozarts were often ill. They had pneumonia, scarlet fever, and even smallpox during their travels. But it never occurred to their father that he might be doing his children harm. He loved them better than anything in the world! He wanted to give them every advantage. And he really thought it his duty to display their God-given talents.

When Wolfgang was fourteen his father took him to Rome. Italy was then the center of the musical world. The best teachers, the best singers, the best operas were in Italy. Indeed, a musician could not call himself "finished" unless he had been to Italy. Young Mozart learned a great deal in Italy because there he had a chance to hear so much fine music. Even a wonder-boy needs to listen. And what a good listener he was!

While he was in Rome, Wolfgang went with his father to hear the Pope's choir sing a very famous old piece of music. This music was one of the treasures of the church and sung only on special occasions. So jealously was it guarded that the singers were forbidden either to take their parts out of the chapel or to copy them. It was very difficult music, with sometimes nine different parts going at once!

Young Mozart had never dreamed of such singing or such music. Every beautiful note of it seemed stamped on his brain. A few nights later his father wakened to find Wolfgang sitting at his desk, fast asleep. He tiptoed over to see what the boy had been doing in the middle of the night, and there on the desk he saw pages and pages of that carefully guarded church music. This amazing boy had written it all down from mere memory!

23

When Frau Mozart, back in Salzburg, read about this in her husband's letter, she was anxious. Both she and Nannerl felt that perhaps it was wicked of Wolfgang to have written down this precious music. But the proud father had not kept it a secret. All Rome knew about it, even the Pope. Instead of being angry with a boy who could do such an unbelievable thing, they were all the more interested in him.

During the next few years, young Mozart visited many cities. When he was twenty-two years old he went again to Paris, this time with his mother as traveling companion. It was a sad tour, for soon after they arrived in Paris the mother became ill and died.

Wolfgang Mozart was no longer an astonishing, charming child, but a grown-up artist. He still gave delightful concerts, but he was becoming even more famous as a composer. His father felt that it was time for him to stop touring and settle down. In those days the only paid musicians were the court musicians and those who played in the houses of rich noblemen. These musicians were looked upon as part of the household staff. They wore servants' uniforms, ate at the servants' table and were ordered about in much the same fashion as the cooks, butlers, and footmen. If the master of the house was generous and a true music lover, his musicians fared well.

Mozart was not fortunate in his master. His father had managed to get him a position in the palace of the Archbishop of Salzburg. Young Mozart did not like it at all. In the first place he was now used to larger cities, and Salzburg's musical life seemed limited and small-townish. He was also used to being treated as a celebrated artist. Imagine how he liked being ordered about by a man who knew little about music! He might be right in the midst of composing an opera or a symphony when he would get an order to pack his belongings and take his musicians down to the Archbishop's country house to entertain the guests! Mozart's father begged him not to be impatient and hot-headed, but it did no good. It was not long before the young musician had quarreled with his master, left his position, and gone to Vienna to try his fortune.

The last part of the Mozart story is almost as hard to believe as that wonderful first part, and sadly different. You can scarcely believe that the man who wrote such priceless music would have to worry about his rent and grocer's bills! But

24

Mozart did. In spite of all his hard work he was miserably poor.

The Emperor, who might have helped him, preferred Italian music and so did little for this German genius. Then too, Mozart had never really had a chance to learn to manage his affairs because his father had always looked after everything. So it was only too easy for dishonest publishers to take his music and then trick him out of the payment he should have had.

To earn money Mozart gave music lessons and played in the rich homes in Vienna. He even wrote tunes for chiming clocks and for the music boxes which were then such a novelty. He was willing to do anything but write poor music. One day a publisher told him that he would not pay him a penny unless he wrote more "popular music"—meaning cheap, catchy tunes. Mozart replied, "Then, my good sir, I shall have to make up my mind to die of hunger!"

But even when life was hard, Mozart was not unhappy. He was merry-hearted like his mother and always expecting things to be better tomorrow. He had a gay young wife and two children, and they seem to have had quite good times in their happy-go-lucky way. Mozart was very generous and often gave away money which he badly needed. He had many friends.

Unfortunately Mozart had never had a strong body. And, of course, all those long, weary journeys and late bedtimes of his childhood had not helped. Besides, he had always worked too hard. His music sounds so fresh and cheerful that we cannot imagine its having anything to do with a headache or a tired back! Artists have a way of giving us only the beauty, and keeping the worry and the weariness to themselves. But never think the artist does not work! A great composer pours out not only the strength of his body, but of his mind and heart as well.

Mozart gave more than his body could afford. One stormy December morning, in the year 1791, Mozart died. The whole musical world was shocked, for he was still a young man. "What might he not have done," people exclaimed, "if only he could have lived a little longer?" No one will ever know. But it seems scarcely possible that even Mozart could have written lovelier music than that which he had already composed.

No one has ever written more beautiful singing melodies. Someone once said, "Mozart taught the instruments to sing," and often, in his orchestra pieces, it does seem as if violins, flutes, clarinets, horns, and all the rest, were voices singing together. And no one has ever been a better musical workman. You will not find ragged phrases or a clutter of useless notes, or one part too big for the other in Mozart's pieces. His music gives the same sort of pleasure we feel when we look at a lovely pattern of lace, a carving, or one of nature's designs in a leaf or a snowflake.

Mozart's music does not try to tell a story or make a picture. Composers of his day simply tried to make beautiful music, full of feeling. Mozart's music is full of the feeling of happiness. As we listen we may imagine a picture, if we like. But most of us are so delighted with the tunes, and the clear and beautiful design, that we forget all about stories and pictures and just enjoy the music itself.

THE LITTLE NOTHINGS

From earliest times the French people have been fond of dancing. French children played dancing games. French peasants made merry with folk dances. And, in the days when life at the French court sounded like something out of a fairy tale, dancing was the royal entertainment. The king and his courtiers danced at their parties. It is said they even mounted the stage at the opera and stepped off their gigues and minuets! French dancing masters were every bit as important as the men who helped rule the country, and French composers were kept busy turning out new dance tunes. So it is not at all surprising that some of the best dance patterns and dance music came from France.

It was the French who began the beautiful dancing on the stage to which we give a French name, *ballet*. At first the ballet dancers followed the pattern of social dances like the minuet or gavotte, which everybody knew. Later the ballet grew into a sort of story dance, with special costumes and scenery that make a wonderful living picture.

When Mozart, aged twenty-two, made his second visit to Paris, a new opera was being planned. It was to begin with a short ballet. The ballet master thought it would be a fine stroke of business to have the music written by the celebrated young German, Wolfgang Mozart. Composer Mozart was very glad to have the business, and set to work on the ballet.

26

This ballet was to have three scenes. In the first, Cupid, the little God of Love, is captured by a troop of young shepherds and shepherdesses, and carried away in a cage tied up with ribbons. The second scene shows the shepherds and shepherdesses playing the game of blindman's buff, to the music of gavottes and minuets. In the last scene Cupid has his revenge. He makes two of the shepherdesses fall in love with the same person, who turns out to be just another shepherdess, disguised as a boy!

It was such a foolish little story that it was called *Les Petite Riens,* which means "The Little Nothings." A set of pieces in Handel and Mozart's time was supposed to have an overture, or opening piece. So, for this ballet music, Mozart wrote an overture so important-sounding that it might be called "A Little Something!" Then followed thirteen short dances— thirteen "little nothings"—for which, unfortunately, he was paid exactly nothing! After a few performances, this ballet was not danced anymore. Mozart's music was laid away for almost a century. When people found it again, they were delighted with these sparkling tunes. They may be called "The Little Nothings," but they are excellent samples of Mozart's charming style.

Pantomime

The "little nothing" called *Pantomime* is from the first scene of the ballet, where Cupid is caught in a net and put in a cage. Probably the young people only wanted to lock up Cupid for a while, so that they could play without being interrupted by any love affairs. Little did they know that a cage meant nothing to Cupid, because he was a god, or that he would later interrupt them with a love affair that would be a good joke!

As you listen to the violins tiptoeing softly:

then running lightly, with little swooping motions:

27

doesn't it make you think of people chasing butterflies with long-handled nets? Certainly this gentle music has no feeling of fear in it. We know that Cupid will not be harmed!

Joyous Gavotte

There are two gavottes in *The Little Nothings*. This is not surprising, for the gavotte was a favorite dance in Mozart's time and became one of music's prettiest patterns. The *gavotte* is an old dance of French mountain peasants called Gavots. The high steps of this mountain dance often seem to be matched by the wide skips in the tune of a gavotte—like this:

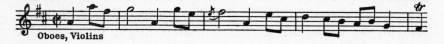
Oboes, Violins

Mozart's gavottes are not quite so high-stepping as the dance of the mountain peasants. But you would scarcely expect stage shepherds and shepherdesses to be quite so rowdy when they were dancing a ballet before the king!

This gavotte, which someone has called the "Joyous Gavotte," must belong to the second scene of the ballet, where the young people are playing blindman's buff. They feel very happy and carefree, for they think they have Cupid locked up and out of mischief.

The music starts out with a gay little whirling, twirling tune:

Allegro

Oboe Violins

Soon it changes, and there is a feeling of dainty kicking and skipping:

As a rest from all this rapid motion, comes a more quiet part beginning with:

Then the first tune comes back and trips joyously to the end
of the dance.

Graceful Gavotte

The second gavotte is called "graceful," because its pretty
rising and falling make us think of dancers bowing and
curtsying:

Violin

There are several little tunes which must belong to different
parts of the dance. All of them are graceful and have the
lovely lines for which Mozart's music is famous.

Minuet—Don Giovanni

Mozart wrote many kinds of music. There were wonderful
long pieces for the orchestra, called symphonies. There were
pieces for smaller groups of instruments and for piano. There
were the plays set to music—the operas. But even in these
larger works we hear little tunes made over the dance patterns
that Mozart loved.

One of the famous Mozart operas is *Don Giovanni,* named
for the hero. In the story, Don Giovanni gives a party at his
palace and his guests dance the popular minuet. If you were
to go to the opera, you would not see this party acted out on
the stage. But you would hear the best part of it, the lovely
dance music, floating out through the open palace windows.

Mozart was living and writing his minuet music in George
Washington's time. It was a time when both men and women
wore powdered wigs and fancy costumes of satin, lace, and
bright-colored velvets. Girls and boys were dressed just like
their elders, and taught to make deep curtsies and gallant
bows. In the candle-lit ballrooms of Old World palaces, and
in New World parlors, people danced the minuet to the
daintiest of music.

The *minuet* is a French dance that always has three beats in
a measure, and usually begins on the first beat. The name of
this dance describes it, for "minuet" means "the dance of the
little steps." In the beginning, the minuet was a country dance
and very lively. But, like so many of the old French dances,

29

when it was borrowed for court dancing the minuet became very dignified indeed.

Although you do not see the dancing at Don Giovanni's party, Mozart's music makes it easy for you to imagine the dancers stepping quietly:

and turning at the end of the phrase:

The music has a second part, beginning:

and ending with a grand bow:

The *Don Giovanni* minuet is good music for dancing as well as for listening. Children still like to dance the minuet and often do it, in old-fashioned costumes, at their George Washington birthday parties.

Romanza from a serenade—EINE KLEINE NACHTMUSIK

A serenade is music made at evening and usually out-of-doors. In Mozart's time serenades were very popular. At the palaces and the houses of rich noblemen, little groups of musicians would entertain the guests by singing and playing out-of-doors on summer evenings. Bands played in the parks and in the village streets. And there was that very special serenader, the lover, singing under his lady's window.

There was also a pretty custom of sending serenaders to a person's house on some special occasion, much as we send flowers. It was a nice way of greeting a returned traveler, a person who had been ill, or someone having a birthday.

Sometimes a serenade was just a simple song or two, or a

piece played by flute and violin or some small group. But again it might be a whole set of pieces written specially for the occasion. Composers were kept busy writing this "night music."

Mozart wrote a number of serenades. The most famous one is this serenade in G major written for a small group of strings. Its title, "A Little Night Music" sounds much prettier when spoken in Mozart's language, *Eine Kleine Nachtmusik.*

This serenade has four parts. The second part, *Romanza,* is the most beautiful. Softly the violins begin to sing:

This music seems to be a part of a warm spring night, like the moonlight and the fragrance of appleblossoms. Just imagine how it would seem to hear it suddenly outside *your* window and know it was *your* serenade! You would surely feel like a little prince or princess, even though you were only plain John or Susie. Lovely music has a way of making us feel rather special.

There are three other little tunes. One begins like this:

Another is a bit livelier:

The last one seems to be a conversation between the first violin and the low strings:

But the beautiful first tune is the favorite. Mozart must have known we would be glad to hear it again. So he used the *rondo,* a pattern in which the first tune keeps coming 'round. We hear it several times before the *Romanza* drifts into its dreamy ending.

3.

Joseph Ghys

Ghent—1801
St. Petersburg—1848

Joseph Ghys was a Belgian violinist who lived more than a hundred years ago. Not much is known about him except that he taught music and played his violin in many cities of Europe.

The few pieces he is said to have written are forgotten, but his name is remembered by an old French tune, *Amaryllis,* which people loved to hear him play. Ghys not only played *Amaryllis* but also rewrote it so that others could play it.

Musicians often do this with old tunes, dressing them up for concert appearance. They sometimes do a special kind of re-writing called *arranging music.* For example, they take a piano piece or an old song and write parts for the instruments of the orchestra to play. Arranging music is not as important as composing a new tune, but it takes a good musician to do it well. Some arrangements are very beautiful. Others change the music so much that we would rather hear it as the composer meant it to sound.

AMARYLLIS

According to the story, *Amaryllis* was composed by a French king about the year 1580. It was first played at the wedding of his daughter, Princess Margaret. No doubt the wedding guests danced to this pretty tune, for the gavotte was a favorite dance at the French court.

The music begins lightly:

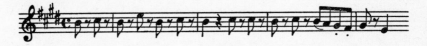

After this skipping tune comes a heavier one in minor mood:

The skipping theme comes back, followed by another tune which sounds as if the dancers were taking little running steps:

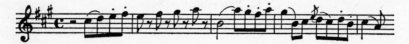

This tune also has a minor partner—the very same tune that followed the skipping theme, but now in a different key. *Amaryllis* has quite a few key changes for such a little piece. And it has two patterns. It is a gavotte and, because the skipping theme keeps coming 'round and 'round, *Amaryllis* is also a rondo.

One morning as I was playing *Amaryllis* my neighbor called out, "Why that's the old ABC song! My father taught me my letters to that tune." But, as I listen to *Amaryllis*, I would rather think of the dancing at Princess Margaret's wedding, wouldn't you?

4.

Franz Schubert

Vienna—1797
Vienna—1828

Once upon a time, and it was a long time ago, there lived on the outskirts of Vienna a poor schoolteacher by the name of Schubert. He had a very large family and a very small house. It was a regular beehive of a house for, added to the swarm of little Schuberts, were all the urchins of Father Schubert's school. There were no public school buildings in those days so these children had to go to the teacher's house for their lessons.

Crowded as it was, the schoolteacher's house was a happy place. There was always room and time for music. The Schubert children learned their notes along with their letters. They could all sing and they loved to experiment with the family instruments—father's cello, brother's fiddle, and the battered old piano which they called the "chopping board."

But the one who sang the sweetest, and whose tiny fingers were cleverest at picking out the tunes, was little Franz. He was their star performer, and the neighbors as well as the family were proud of him. Brother Ignaz gave him piano lessons, father taught him fiddling, and the village choirmaster was his singing teacher. Franz was too good! He learned so quickly that they did not know what to do with him. The choirmaster said he had never had such a pupil. "When I begin to teach him something new, I find that he knows it already!"

Father Schubert was at his wit's end. Here he was with a genius for a son and not a dollar to spare for his education! Fortunately there was in Vienna a famous old school called the *Konvikt,* where a chosen group of boys were given their living and schooling, music included, in exchange for their services in the Emperor's choir. Franz had a sweet, clear voice and could read any music at sight. One day his father saw this advertisement:"Boy-soprano wanted: must be in good health and must have got over the smallpox." He decided that Franz should try for the job.

A crowd of eager boys came for the tryout, some boasting how good they were, others frankly scared. All were excited because they had heard that the court choirmaster who was to examine them was a very exacting musician and not above pulling the ears of a boy who sang flat! Into this group slipped Franz, a queer little figure with a mop of black curls and big steel spectacles that gave him an owlish look. Although he was eleven years old, he was small for his age and looked even more childish in the faded blue-gray smock his mother had made for him. The other boys laughed, called him "little miller," and asked him what he thought he was doing there! But when it came to singing the difficult test pieces and answering the questions of the examiners, the stumpy little miller left the laughers far behind. He was one of three boys chosen to wear the brave gold-laced uniform of the Imperial Chapel.

Franz spent five years at the *Konvikt*. They were war years. Food and money were scarce. The bleak old *Konvikt* building was cold and the boys were given but two scant meals a day. Little Schubert wrote hungry letters begging the home folks to send him a few extra pennies, so that he might buy an apple now and then.

He was not unhappy. Life in Vienna in those days was anything but dull. Getting up each morning was like turning the page in an exciting story book! And although his stomach may have been a bit empty, Franz's head and heart were full of music. Besides the singing, the boys at the *Konvikt* school had a little orchestra which met every evening after supper. Franz was made first violinist and later, when the leader was absent, he acted as director.

All the while he was secretly scribbling music of his own on every scrap of paper he could find. During recreation hours he would slip off to hear how it sounded on the piano in the icy music room. It was a happy day for him when an older boy found him there, coaxed him to go on playing, and then kindly offered to supply him with real music paper.

Sunday afternoons and holidays Franz spent with his family. They always played quartets—the beautiful music of Haydn, Mozart, and Beethoven which they so dearly loved. It is a

36

pleasant picture of home life, the two older brothers with their violins, Franz with the viola, and the father sawing earnestly away on his cello. Father Schubert sometimes made mistakes which, at a wink from the older boys, Franz would tactfully correct. After a while Franz began bringing home quartets he had written. On one grand occasion he brought a piece for three boys' voices, with guitar accompaniment, which he had written for his father's birthday!

So the years passed. When school days were over, young Franz had to take his place in the world. There was not much of a living to be made from music in those days, so when his father suggested that he follow the family profession of school-teaching, Franz agreed to try to teach the younger children in the Schubert school. He was a dismal failure! He liked children and was kind to them, but their droning voices and grubby little slates bored him unspeakably! His whole heart was in his music, in the lovely songs and quartets which he spent every spare moment writing.

One day two of his old school friends came to visit him and found him correcting a pile of children's copybooks. They decided that it was all wrong for a fellow like Schubert, who might be one of the best composers, to waste his time being the worst of teachers. So they simply carried him off! One of them, a rich young man whose mother had a large house, gave Schubert a home. The other friend set out to advertise Schubert's music by giving parties at which it could be played and sung. He knew that no matter how beautifully a composer may write, he can never get anywhere unless what he writes is heard and published.

It was not long before Schubert and his music had many friends and admirers in Vienna. This made Schubert very happy for he was a warmhearted, sociable fellow. But in spite of all his friends could do, Schubert never had any luck with publishers. They either refused to buy his music or paid him only a few cents for pieces from which they were later to make thousands of dollars. Although Schubert a wrote a great deal of music—hundreds of songs, piano pieces, quartets and symphonies—very little of it was printed until after his death.

He was always poor, so poor that he often lacked proper food and clothes. It is sad to think that this friendly, hard-working man should have been so neglected. But Schubert seldom complained. He went bravely to the parties in his shabby old clothes, and kept on writing the lovely songs and symphonies. He gave up the thought of a home of his own because he was too poor to marry. But he was always so cheery that few people ever knew his disappointment. His friends and his music were his riches, and in them he found real happiness.

Schubert spent his whole life in or near Vienna. It was a short life, for he died when he was only thirty-one. But in that short lifetime, Schubert gave to the world enough beautiful melodies to keep us happy all our lives long.

MARCHE MILITAIRE

This is a stern-sounding title which might make us expect to hear stern-sounding music. What a surprise it is when the orchestra begins to play Schubert's *Marche Militaire!* Surely this lighthearted, prancing tune does not suggest the sober business of war. It sounds more like a parade. That is just what it is meant to be, a musical snapshot of the Emperor's body-guard riding through the streets of old Vienna.

They were soldiers, to be sure, and doubtless, somewhere underneath all their buttons and gold lace, they carried brave enough hearts. But they were show soldiers, young fellows from rich families who could afford the buttons and gold lace, the plumed helmets, the silver-mounted harness, the satiny horses, and the servants to keep them all so shining. They were picked men, chosen for their good looks and perfectly drilled for their parts in the military pageant which was supposed to represent a nation's greatness. The uglier parts of that pageant, the messy bleeding and dying, were played by less shiny fellows.

The people of Vienna loved to see these show soldiers parade and drill, and who wouldn't! I shall never forget the two regiments of show soldiers I saw drilling on the old Crusaders' tournament ground outside the city of Berlin. One regiment was all white and silver, white uniforms, white horses, silver trimmings and silver pennants. The other regiment was black and gold. As they came dashing down the field I felt as if some King Arthur legend was coming to life before my eyes. Men and horses were so beautiful they seemed scarcely real. And oh, the drummers! Two were white and silver, two were black and gold. Each man had a pair of kettledrums, one on each

38

side of his saddle bow. The reins were fastened to the drummer's feet so that his hands might be free for playing. And at the slightest pull on the reins the perfectly trained horses reared until they stood almost upright, and, if you can believe me, balanced themselves like statue horses while the rhythmic drum beats set the company of soldiers wheeling.

No wonder shabby little Franz Schubert gaped and thrilled as he watched the Imperial Guards go through their parade drills. And because Schubert's thrills always turned into tunes, he later wrote his *Marche Militaire,* which he dedicated to the regiment that had inspired it.

As you listen to this music, imagine yourself a little boy of old Vienna. It is a bright, tingling morning in September. The schoolteacher has given you a half holiday because it is the Emperor's birthday and the Imperial Guards are to parade. You hurry off with Wilhelm and Peter to get a good place. What a lot of people! The streets are full, the steps are full, the balconies and windows are full of people. Policemen, like giant mechanical toys, are doing their best to trim the edges of the crowd into a tidy line.

"Oh, dear! I wish we could have found a place nearer the palace! It's such fun to see the big gates swing open and spill the parade out into the square!"

"Well, we can't get down there through this crowd! And besides, there goes the tower clock striking eleven—they'll be coming any minute now!"

"Yes! There are the drums!"

(The whole orchestra turns itself into a big drum.)
"And there's the music!"

"How far away it sounds. I can't hear!"

"Oh, stop fussing, Wilhelm, I can't hear so very well either, but they'll play it over and over. Now it's getting closer.—Now it's grand and loud!"

"Here they come! Here they come!"

"Oh, look, Peter, the horses are keeping time to the music! They are too!"

"Aren't the flags grand! Don't you just love that light blue color! When I grow up I'm going to be one of the Emperor's guards."

"I'll bet you won't! My father says it costs hundreds and thousands and millions—"

"Oh, look! They're passing that balcony full of ladies! And listen, the band is playing a ladies' tune, sort of soft and fluttery:

The ladies are waving their kerchiefs and blowing kisses. They look pretty, don't they?"

"Did you see the man just behind the officer salute? I'll bet his girl's up there!"

"A fellow would feel pretty smart to have his girl see him in a parade like this, wouldn't he?"

"Now they're playing the other tune again. I like it best, it's so nice and drummy! You can always feel the beats: *Tump ta, ta, tump, tump; tump ta, ta, tump, tump.*"

"Do you suppose we could go down to the parade ground and watch them drill for just a little while?"

"Of course not, there's the clock playing the three-quarters tune already!"

"Well, I think Herr Becker might have given us the whole day off, the old stingy!"

"Peter, I'll bet you can't whistle that tune they marched to!"

"I'll bet I can."

It all happened more than a hundred years ago. The crack regiment, the old Emperor, and the little boys are long gone. But Schubert's music marches right along through the years with all its flags flying, a gallant company of picked tones!

40

Part Two

STORY AND
PICTURE MUSIC

THE EARLY composers, as you know, were quite satisfied to express their feelings—and ours—in beautiful tone patterns. For this pattern music they let us make our own stories and pictures. But styles change, in music as in everything else. Later composers wanted us to imagine *their* story or picture, as well as our own. So they gave their pieces titles like *The Dancing Doll* and *Dreaming*.

There is a key word which belongs to the idea of story and picture music. It is the word "suggest." *To suggest* is to make a person think of something without telling him all about it. This lets the other person have a part in the idea. Poets, painters, and composers know that most of us like to do some of the imagining, for then the story or picture is partly ours.

It's like this. Suppose a painter has made a picture of little girls playing ring-around-a-rosy in a field. As I look at it, I see exactly what the painter wanted me to see—children playing in a field. But I also see something else. I see a pattern of circles—a ring of little girls with round faces and wheels of whirling skirts, little round daisies in the grass, round white clouds in the sky, and even a half-circle of trees watching in the background. I think how clever it was of the painter to choose a pattern of circles for this picture.

Another artist has made a pretty wallpaper pattern of circling lines, pale blue and pink and lavender lines, on a soft green background. I choose it for my bedroom. One morning, as I am looking at my new wallpaper, I suddenly say, "Why, that pattern makes me think of little girls playing ring-around-a-rosy in a field." The artist probably never thought of such a thing as he made his pretty pattern of circles. But an artist's work may suggest all sorts of ideas to those who enjoy it.

41

We know that music cannot tell a story as words do, or paint a picture in lines and colors that our real eyes can see. Music can only suggest—make us think of a story or picture. And there can be many different imaginary stories and pictures for the same piece. There is no right and wrong to the way people think and feel about music.

Often a story that music suggests seems even more real than one that is told in words. This is because the music not only lets you help make the story, but also gives you the very feeling of it. A few bars of Schubert's *Marche Militaire* takes you right to the parade. You get the feeling of those prancing horses and of the excited little boys keeping time with the music. Why, for a moment you are one of those little boys! People who share the same feelings can be very close to each other, even though they may be hundreds of miles and hundreds of years apart!

Music has many ways of suggesting. One of the best is by rhythm, for it can march, dance, sway, and make us think of everything from soldiers to sleepy babies. Melody, too, can suggest. A tune that seems to climb up makes us think of gay and lively things. One that droops suggests quiet things, drowsiness or even sadness. And there is harmony—tones sounding together to make the major and minor moods, which are the light and shadow of music.

Story and picture music is full of clever uses of fast and slow, loud and soft, high and low. The different instrument voices are good at suggesting. The flute can trill like a bird or the double bass can lumber along like an elephant. But a composer has to be very careful with his suggesting and not get to imitating. If he tries to make a piece sound exactly like a boiler factory or a barnyard, he just makes noise, not music. Music must always have beautiful tones and tone patterns.

Now you see why we speak of pattern music and story and picture music—just to show you the two slightly different kinds of music. In one, the composer's main idea is to express feeling in a beautiful pattern of tones; in the other, he wants to suggest a particular story or picture. Good listeners enjoy both kinds of music and they soon discover that there is not so much difference between the two. As you listen, remember that, whether a piece is called *Romanza* or *The Enchanted Lake,* the really important thing is that it is beautiful music.

42

5.

Robert Schumann

Zwickau—1810
Endenich—1856

If you were to visit Zwickau, Germany, today, you would see a bustling, modern city. The big factories and busy shops, the trains and motor cars rushing about would make you think of our American cities. You could hardly believe that Zwickau is an old, old city, mentioned in books that were written two hundred years before Columbus started out to find the New World!

Zwickau once had a great wall around it. Outside the wall was a wide, deep ditch filled with water, called a "moat." In times of war the townspeople drew up the bridges over the moat and barred the big gates in the wall. This made them quite safe as long as their food lasted. But if the enemy kept them shut up inside the wall until everything was eaten up, then old General Hunger nearly always won the fight.

In 1810, when our story begins, the walls of Zwickau had been torn down and the moat filled up. In their place were beautiful gardens, circling this old part of the town like a giant wreath. Nearby ran the broad Mulde river. There were also three huge ponds in which people could fish and hunt water fowl. And there were fairy-tale forests on all sides. Zwickau was a pleasant place in which to live.

One of the most interesting places in the town was the book-shop kept by Herr August Schumann. Herr Schumann was not the kind of shopkeeper who sells books as if they were bricks or sausages. He really loved books for the knowledge and the pleasure he got from them. As a boy he had wanted more than anything in the world to go to college and learn to write books. Instead he had gone to work in a grocery, because his father was too poor to send him to college.

But August Schumann did not bury his hopes in sugar and

43

meal! Every evening he would hurry home to his books. He even taught himself to read French and English books! Then he began to write stories and had the luck to sell one of them. With this money he started to college. Alas, it wasn't enough money, and soon August had to go back to work. This time he found a position in a bookshop. He liked it so much that as soon as he could he started a bookshop in partnership with his brother. He not only sold books but printed and published them, and every little while he would write a book himself.

One day, in the summer of 1810, the people of Zwickau read in their newspapers: "Born on the 8th of June, to Herr August Schumann, notable citizen and bookseller, a little son." Not one of those readers thought that this was very important news. But it was—more important than the news of Napoleon, who was trying to rule all of Europe, even Germany. For this little son was not just one more pink baby, of which the town had plenty. This was Robert Schumann, whose music was to make the whole world glad, long after Napoleon's troops were forgotten.

Robert was the youngest of the five Schumann children and the family pet. His mother could not bear to say "No" to this baby. She called him her little *Lichtpunkt,* her bright spot. And the older children were quite sure that no one else had such a dear little blue-eyed brother. To tell the plain truth, Robert Schumann was spoiled.

But it was the father who was most proud of the boy. Little Robert learned more quickly than the others. He seemed to have a great love for books and music. "Ah," thought August Schumann, "this is my very own dream child. He shall have a chance to do the things I wanted to do when I was a boy." When Robert was six, he was sent to a good school. And he had music lessons from the church organist, who was the best musician in the town.

August Schumann's shop was a wonderful place for a boy like Robert to spend his time. He became a regular bookworm, reading stories, travel books, plays and poetry. He liked the poetry best of all. When he was tired of reading he would go back into the print shop and watch them making books. He learned to read those long strips they print first to see if the type is set right. Those strips are called printer's proof. Robert was proud of his proofreading and, as he grew older, he was

44

quite a help in the printing room, and spent much time there.

Robert Schumann was one of those children who love to make things. Almost as soon as he could read, he was trying to make stories and music of his own. He wrote childish poems and "robber plays," which the children performed. When he was only seven years old, he made little dances which he played on the piano. This greatly pleased his father.

There was not much chance to hear music in Zwickau, except in church. The town band played on all public occasions, but a boy could learn little from its music. So when Robert was nine, his father took him to a neighboring city to hear a concert by a famous pianist. Robert never forgot that wonderful evening. It made him work harder than ever at his own music.

He got together a little orchestra of schoolboys. There were two violins, two flutes, a clarinet, two horns, and Robert at the piano. In the bookshop Robert found some sheets of orchestra music from which they could play. Some of the parts were missing, but he filled in these gaps at the piano. When the players needed new pieces, Robert wrote them. Herr Schumann presented the orchestra with eight new music racks. He also presented himself as an audience at their concerts. How this one-man audience could applaud!

Robert and his friends had good times with their music. One of the things they enjoyed most was to have Robert sit down at the piano and make "musical portraits" for them. He could make tunes picture a lazy boy, a stern old man, or a pretty little girl, so clearly that the listeners could nearly always guess the person he was thinking of. Years later, when Schumann was a real composer, he made a wonderful set of musical pictures called *Carnaval,* with twenty-two short piano pieces picturing Schumann's young friends at a masked ball.

August Schumann knew that his son's greatest talent was for music. He felt that it must have every chance to develop. When Robert had finished school in Zwickau, his father meant to send him away to study with a really fine music teacher. But before Robert was ready for this important next step, his dear father died. How the boy missed this man who had shared and helped with every fine thing he had ever done! Robert felt lost. He had always been a dreamy boy, and now he grew more quiet than ever. He read a great deal of fanciful poetry which

45

helped to carry him off into a romantic world of make-believe.

When Robert was eighteen and ready for college, his mother scarcely knew what to do with him. He was still her darling, her *Lichtpunkt*. She wanted him to have a happy life. She too was proud of his music, but she thought he should have some other way of earning a living, like being a lawyer. Who would pay a man for dreaming at a piano? So, to please his mother, Robert, the dreamer, went off to law school.

He went first to Leipzig, then on to the beautiful old university town of Heidelberg. Robert loved Heidelberg. The wooded mountains and the banks of the river Rhine were perfect for long walks. In the ruins of the famous old castle, he could picture the knights who used to live there and have such exciting adventures. He spent happy evenings with other young people who liked music and poetry. He also spent too much money. No ordinary student's room was good enough for this young man. He had to have rooms large enough for a grand piano and for the supper parties he liked to give. And he was quite sure he needed holiday trips to Italy and other interesting places. His guardian sent money, his mother sent money, even his brothers and sisters sent money to Robert. It is no wonder that he never in his life knew how to value it, for it had come to him too easily!

It was not all play at Heidelberg. Robert worked, but it was at music, not law. He seldom went to the law classes and when he did his thoughts were miles away. He could not bear the dry law books full of what he called "icy-cold definitions." He did not want to learn how to settle other people's quarrels. He wanted to be a concert pianist. Finally, after two years, he wrote to his mother begging to be allowed to give up the law. Frau Schumann then wrote a letter to Robert's old music teacher in Leipzig. She asked the teacher, Herr Wieck, if he thought her son had musical talent enough to become a successful concert pianist. Herr Wieck wrote back that Robert had plenty of talent if only he would stop dreaming and do some of the hard work it takes to make a real artist. Robert, of course, promised to work like a slave. His mother let him have his way.

Robert Schumann was twenty years old when he went back to Leipzig to *work* at music. He began to study piano with Herr Wieck and, for a while, lived in his teacher's house. He was a great favorite with the Wieck children. They had never known anyone who could think up such good riddles or tell such shivery ghost stories as young Herr Schumann. And he could teach little boys the most marvelous tricks. He had good piano tricks, too, and could make pictures and stories in music. Father Wieck's tunes never did anything half so nice!

The most interesting of the Wieck children was Clara. She was only twelve years old when Schumann came to live at the Wieck house, but she was her father's star piano pupil. He had already begun to take her on concert tours. Robert Schumann was amazed to find that a little girl could play so well. He liked her, too, for she was sweet and friendly and full of fun. When she was away they would write letters. Clara would tell Robert about her concerts and he would tell her what the children had been doing. He liked to write foolish questions such as, "How do the apples taste in Frankfurt?" When Clara was at home they went for long tramps together and played duets on winter evenings.

Schumann was now working hard at his music. Every day he practiced at the piano for hours. He was so eager to train his fingers that he rigged up a sort of harness to hold up the weak fourth finger while the other fingers played. It was a foolish stunt and lamed his right hand so badly that the doctors said he could never be a concert pianist! He was very brave about this and wrote his mother, "Don't be anxious about my finger. I can compose without it." Perhaps the lame hand was not such a misfortune after all. Who of us would have known Robert Schumann if he had been only a piano player, with little time for writing music? Surely the good fairies who left the gifts of poetry and music in Robert Schumann's cradle meant him to be a composer!

Schumann was quite happy with his composing. He studied the music of the great masters, Bach and Beethoven. He learned all the things composers must know, and he wrote a great deal. Soon musicians began to notice this young Schumann and his music.

There was in Leipzig a little restaurant called the *Kaffeebaum*, "The Coffee Tree." Here the younger artists used to meet and talk for hours about music. They had many new ideas which they thought much better than those of the "old fogy" musicians who were running the music schools and the orchestras. Schumann and his friends decided to tell the world what they thought about music. So they started a music magazine and made Schumann its editor. It was just the kind of thing he could do, for he had always used words almost as well as he used tones. In this new music magazine he wrote such interesting things about the old composers that people hunted up their music and began to enjoy it more than ever. And he wrote so much in praise of the young and unknown composers that people began to say, "Who is this fellow, Chopin?" and "Who is this Brahms boy from Hamburg? Let's hear some of their music if it's so good." This was exactly what Schumann and his friends hoped would happen. They wanted fine old music to be remembered, and new music to have a chance to be heard.

During these busy years little Clara Wieck had been growing up. She was seventeen now and a famous pianist. She and Robert were still the same good comrades, tramping and playing together, and exchanging funny letters. Then one day Robert made a discovery. Several times he had fancied himself in love with some pretty lady, but it would soon be all over. Now he found that there was a girl who was always in his thoughts, a girl he really loved. He wanted to marry her. It was all quite surprising because this girl was his old comrade Clara—Clara who for years had seemed like a dear little sister! And Clara felt just the same way about Robert.

Father Wieck would not hear of such a thing. He liked Robert Schumann and thought him a brilliant young musician, but he didn't want his Clara to marry anyone. If she had a husband, a home, and children to think about, what would become of those concert tours that brought fame and money to the Wiecks? He made a terrible fuss, and for several years everyone was very unhappy. But when Clara was twenty-one, and could do as she pleased, she and Robert were married.

Robert and Clara Schumann had a fine life together. Robert was proud of Clara's playing and often went with her on her concert tours. Clara knew that Robert was a great composer, and was proud to play his music. This famous pianist and great composer were just as proud to be the mother and father of the seven Schumann children. They had a happy home.

The Schumanns lived for a while in Dresden. Later they went to Düsseldorf, a city on the Rhine. Here Schumann was conductor of the orchestra and of the singers club. He was not a very good conductor. He just couldn't be strict enough when men were late or played wrong notes. And he was such a dreamer that sometimes he forgot to give his players their signals. You can imagine what that did to the performance!

Frederick Niecks, who has written many books about music, was a little boy in Düsseldorf when Schumann lived there. He says, "I remember very well my father pointing Schumann out to me as he was slowly walking by himself in the public park. I can still see the quiet face, the rounded lips, as if he were whistling, and the dreamy, faraway look."

The children of Düsseldorf were not long to see this kindly, quiet man walking in their park. Schumann had lived there only four years when a terrible illness struck him. The dreams from which he had made such beautiful music now seemed to become tangled in his poor brain. He heard one tone singing in his ears day and night. Then little tunes came and would not let him sleep. After a while he could remember nothing. One dark, rainy day he was so unhappy that he ran out of his house and threw himself in the river. Boatmen pulled him out and brought him home.

After that he was taken to a hospital in the country. Everyone hoped that the quiet and fresh air might cure him. But Robert Schumann never came back. His children never saw him again. For two years he lived in a dream world. Poor Clara Schumann had to travel about, giving concerts to earn money for her children.

This was the time when young Johannes Brahms was such a wonderful friend to the Schumanns. He stayed with the children and cheered them while their mother was away. He made the sad visits to the hospital to see that everything was being done for the sick man. And, when it was all over, young Brahms walked in front of the sorrowful little procession of friends who took Robert Schumann to an old cemetery by the Star Gate in Bonn.

SCENES FROM CHILDHOOD
Kinderscenen

Robert Schumann was a happy child. He had a loving mother and father, jolly sisters and brothers, and a pleasant home. There were books and music to brighten the indoor

49

hours. There were the inviting parks and ponds of Zwickau for out-of-door play. And if the Schumann children felt like "foreign travel," there were the woods, the meadows, the river, and old *Windberg*, the "Windy Mountain," waiting just outside the town.

Best of all, there was Robert's own fairy gift of fancy. This gift is called "imagination." It is indeed a fairy gift, for it can often change a sorry, ugly thing into something lovely. Most of you have this gift. You should be careful not to lose it! If you can only keep your happy fancies, you will always have one of the nicest parts of your childhood. You will never be *too old*, not even when your hair is snow-white!

Robert Schumann kept his fairy gift all his life long. Just a little while before his marriage, his sweetheart, Clara, told him that sometimes he seemed to her like a child. This made him think of those pleasant years in Zwickau. He could picture that little Robert playing games, reading story books, watching the flames dance in the fireplace, and then falling fast asleep. Schumann's fancies always found their way into music. And so these memories of his childhood became little music pictures.

He wrote to Clara about them. In his letter he said, "I felt as if I had wings. I wrote thirty droll little pieces from which I have chosen twelve and called them *Scenes from Childhood*. You will like them." Then he told her that when she played them she must forget that she was a famous pianist. She must fancy herself a little girl again. These pieces belong to childhood. They cannot be played or even enjoyed by people who have lost their fairy gift.

Schumann's mind was full of pictures and stories and fanciful thoughts. He hardly knew whether to tell these thoughts in words or tones. Even when he chose tones, a word or two would nearly always slip into the title. He was one of the first composers to give picture titles to his music.

There is something very queer and very nice about Schumann's titles. They were chosen *after* the music was written! At first the *Scenes from Childhood* were just nameless little tunes, some lively, some quiet. They only gave the feelings a child might have. Then Schumann sat down at his piano and played them over and over until his fancy said, "Why, this merry, running tune sounds like children playing tag," or, "Now the child must be falling asleep." So, you see, Schumann's tunes really chose their own names. Perhaps that is why they have such nice names!

As we listen to this music we can feel ourselves running in the game of tag or almost falling asleep. The music and the pictures seem to be our very own. The composer wanted us to feel just this way. Music we love and understand always seems to be our very own.

It is pleasant to imagine that we are the heroes of all these music pictures, but it is not quite fair to forget Robert. *Scenes from Childhood* are really pictures of a little boy who lived more than a hundred years ago. They were made by the child himself, after he had become a great composer.

About Strange Lands and People

The first two pieces from *Scenes from Childhood* make us think of Robert Schumann in his father's bookshop. We can see a little boy turning the pages of a big travel book. What does it matter if there are strange words he cannot understand? There are pictures, and there are maps of all the foreign lands —patches of green and pink and yellow, lying in a blue sea. A child can go a-journeying with his finger all the way around the world! And, as he sails into those pink and yellow ports, he will see strange sights and strange-looking people.

These faraway thoughts bring faraway feelings. The faraway feelings steal into the music. It is almost as if we heard a voice calling:

and echoing:

from those strange lands.

For a moment the music sounds nearer:

Then it drifts back again to that soft, far call. The picture, never clear, is just a passing thought about strange lands and people.

51

There is nothing dreamy or faraway about this piece. Schumann called it *Curious Story,* and it must have been a jolly story. That romping first tune:

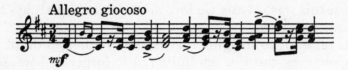

might have come from some happy hobgoblin. Or it might belong to scuffling boys or dogs having a wild play in a vacant lot.

There is a second tune which is much more quiet:

You will notice that composers nearly always put a quiet tune after a lively one. It is a good idea, for it gives a restful change of feeling. This quiet tune also has a place in the story. There must be some quiet moments even in a hobgoblin's life!

After a little rest, back comes the first tune. It seems livelier than ever since we have heard the quiet tune.

No one knows just what story Schumann was thinking of when he wrote this music. He did not tell because he wanted each listener to make his own curious story. Wouldn't it be interesting to read all the different stories this tune has suggested in the many years people have been listening to it?

Catch Me if You Can!

Surely no child who ever played tag could miss the meaning of this piece. Away go the notes on lightly running feet:

There is not a quiet moment in this music. One wouldn't dare pause to rest in the middle of a game of tag! Even the second tune races along:

It teases:

You know how a good tag player pauses just long enough to puzzle the other fellow, then darts off in quite another direction.

The orchestra plays a much better game of tag than the piano, because it has so many more players. You will hear one instrument starting the game, another running in after it. Even the soft sticks that cannot play a tune can tap in their excitement.

It is a good game for woodwinds. The brasses are too heavy for such racing. And the poor strings are usually kept so busy making the accompaniment that they get no chance to play!

The Pleading Child

If ever a tune seemed to be asking for something, this one does. Do you know what makes it sound that way? It is that little upward turn at the end of the phrase. When you say "May I?" your voice does not go down at the end, as it does when you say "Good morning!" It tilts up at the end because you are not sure that you will get what you are asking for.

This little tune does just the same thing. It tilts up at the end in a question:

All the "asking" would go out of it if it went like this:

The child keeps on pleading:

and he promises to be so good:

Then we hear the first tune again and, at the very end, the child's voice goes way up, in such a pretty "Please!"

Please

How hard it would be to say "No" to a child who asks so sweetly! Few people ever did say "No" to Robert Schumann!

Happy Enough

This little tune seems to be all smiles:

It is so happy that every now and then it has to hop and skip:

Children hippity-hop like that on their way to the circus or to buy ice cream.

Happiness does seem to make you feel light. It lifts you right up! And now it lifts this tune, too. You can hear it go up into a higher key, then come gently down again.

You can't help thinking that the child has been given what he was asking for in the last piece. It must have been something very nice to make a child so happy!

Important Event

This title sounds more like a newspaper headline than the name of a piece of music. Those are not a child's words. Yet there are many important events in a child's life. "Event," you know, means a "happening," but not just an everyday happening. We call it an event only when a thing happens for the first time, or when it happens just once in a long while. But it is an event when you put on your first long trousers, when you go on the train alone, or hold the new baby. As we listen to this music we might picture a small boy in very new shoes going somewhere with Father. He feels manly. He walks heavily.

Robert Schumann often went places with his father. You may remember that when Robert was nine years old, the two of them went to a town miles away to hear a great artist play on the piano. That was an important event.

How different this music feels from the other pieces! These notes do not run and skip. They are all piled up in neat little chord stacks. They move heavily:

And how important the bass grows:

as if to say, "Things like this do not happen every day!"

Dreaming

This is a very famous piece. You will hear it played at concerts and over the radio many times. You will often hear it played on the violin, for the smooth, singing tone of the violin seems just right for *Dreaming*. Everybody loves this piece. But not everybody knows that it is one of Schumann's *Scenes from Childhood*. And not everybody knows that its real name, *Traumerei*, is just the German way of saying "dreaming."

Softly the tones rise, then come floating down again as gently as snowflakes:

Can you hear how Schumann keeps tilting the tune upward, even as it falls? That is why it sounds so dreamy. Dreams never have ruler lines with hard edges. They are soft and feathery.

Sometimes when our thoughts are far away, we seem to be dreaming even though we are not asleep. We call this daydreaming. We do not know whether the child in this picture is asleep or just daydreaming. But whichever it is, it is a beautiful dream. This music always brings a beautiful daydream and quiet thoughts. That is why everybody loves *Dreaming*.

By the Fireside

Sitting by the fireside is drowsy business. The heat in your face and the flames wavering before your eyes make you feel so sleepy! So when you hear of a piece called *By the Fireside*, you expect drowsy music.

Schumann's *By the Fireside* is a surprise. It is no drowsy tune. It leaps and dances:

and toward the end, crackles merrily:

A child would love to watch a jolly fire like this. If he had a handful of pine cones to toss in, what a gay popping there would be and what a nice, spicy smell! And if the child used his fairy gift of fancy he might see the little fire imps at play. Every now and then they send up fireworks, Roman candle sparks, that twinkle up the sooty chimney. Sometimes you can hear them singing a queer little hissing song. How lightly they can dance! What a pity to fall asleep and miss such a frolic!

Knight of the Hobbyhorse

Here comes a knight on horseback. In olden times the knights were men who were supposed to go about rescuing people. They wore those queer metal suits you can see in art museums.

This knight is in a great hurry. He must be rushing off to help some fair doll in distress:

But there is something a little odd about this horse. Let your body go with the music. It rocks, doesn't it, back and forth— back and forth. Now can you guess the secret? Yes, it is a hobby-horse on wooden rockers!

You can hear those rockers and you can see them too. (I have marked the rocker notes with dotted lines.) The tune just rocks back and forth between those notes. Notice how hard it rocks. It thumps down on the last note in each right-hand measure. This knight is getting nowhere fast, but he seems quite cheerful!

Almost Too Serious

What could a little boy be thinking about to make him feel so serious? Is he thinking how long it is until next Christmas? Or is he wondering where the stars stay in the daytime, or why people who live on the under side of the round world don't fall off?

The music seems to be wondering too:

It is not at all sure sounding. The listener wonders whether it is going to stop at the end of every phrase.

It is a pretty tune but—*almost too serious*.

Frightening

Have you ever heard a poem called "Shadow March"? It is a poem by Robert Louis Stevenson about a little boy who was afraid to go to bed. He lived in an old house of tall stairs and long, dark hallways. It was in the days of flickering candlelight. When the little boy started on his bedtime journey, his own cozy room seemed miles away. He tried to be brave but, as he climbed the dark stairs, great crooked shadows came out and marched along behind him!

> The shadow of the baluster, the shadow of the lamp,
> The shadow of the child that goes to bed,
> All the wicked shadows coming, tramp, tramp, tramp,
> With the black night overhead.

Schumann must have been thinking of just such a scary adventure when he wrote *Frightening*.

At first the music sounds anxious:

It makes you think of Stevenson's little boy with his candle. He dreads that long, black journey, but he is trying to be brave. Perhaps if he walks on tiptoe, the bogey will not hear him!

But it is no use. Out jump the shadows:

How swiftly they move, but how softly!

All the way through, we hear the bogey tune pouncing upon

58

the little anxious tune. There is not a safe moment in the whole piece until the very end. Then the music sounds comfortable:

The little boy has reached his own bright room and closed the door on frightening shadows!

Child Falling Asleep

Now the music begins to nod:

We hear a sweet voice:

as if the dream fairy were calling to the tired child.

The whole world seems to be rocking and nodding until at last even the music itself falls asleep before it reaches a finishing chord.

The Poet Speaks

This last picture is the most fanciful of all. As I listen to this music I seem to see a door opening softly. Someone slips in and stands looking down at the sleeping child. I like to think that it is Robert Schumann, the poet-composer, looking down at Robert Schumann, the child. Strange thoughts come to him. Can it be true that this little knight of the hobbyhorse is the same person who is soon to marry Clara Wieck! Why, this foolish little person has not yet learned not to be afraid of shadows!

But do not smile, Big Robert, are you not afraid sometimes?

You may not be afraid of shadows on the stairs, but there are other kinds of shadows now. Perhaps that little boy is not so far away after all. Childhood is very real and very near to thoughtful people.

The music is thoughtful:

Adagio espressivo

and, at its quiet ending, the poet disappears and the door closes on the sleeping child.

Schumann was always fond of his *Scenes from Childhood*. He often played them for his own children. Another great musician, Franz Liszt, loved these little pieces. In a letter to a friend, Liszt writes, "Every evening before the children go to bed, I play *Scenes from Childhood* for them." And, like the Liszt and Schumann children of so long ago, hundreds of today's children love to listen to *Scenes from Childhood*. You too?

6.

Georges Bizet

Paris—1838
Bougival—1875

Alexandre César Léopold was the name the Bizets gave to their little boy. But the baby's godfather did not like this grand name and kept calling the boy Georges, until Georges he became to his family and to the world.

From his babyhood little Georges' ears were tuned to music. The Bizet house rang with it from morning until night, for the father was a singing teacher and the mother a pianist. Georges' parents were determined to make a musician of their little son. When he was only four his mother began to guide the fat baby fingers over the piano keys. Then the father took him in hand and was amazed to find that his tiny pupil already knew many songs and singing exercises. Georges had been having a keyhole course of his own, outside his father's studio door!

When he was only nine years old he entered the special music school called the Paris Conservatory. Rarely had that famous old school seen such a student as little Bizet. He could play the piano and organ beautifully, and he was already clever at writing music. Georges won prize after prize. He also won everybody's heart. He was such a handsome, laughing youngster, with his mop of yellow curls, his dancing eyes, and sturdy body.

At the Paris Conservatory there is a very special prize in composition called the *Prix de Rome,* the prize of Rome. It is an old prize and generations of students have dreamed of winning it. To win this prize means not only great honor, but the chance to live and study in Italy. Nineteen-year-old Georges Bizet tried for the *Prix de Rome* and won it.

It was a great day in the Bizet family when Georges started for Rome. He spent three happy years in Italy studying and writing music. The letters he wrote home are full of the good times he was having with other students in that beautiful country. In those same letters he tells his father and mother that when he comes home they will not need to work and give music lessons any longer. He is going to write operas that will make him rich and famous. "A hundred thousand francs," he wrote, "why, it is nothing!"

Poor Georges! His happy dreams did not come true. He returned from Rome to find his dear mother was dead. And as for the money he was to earn, few composers have worked so hard and made so little. He had no luck with his operas. You will remember that operas are plays in which the actors sing their parts instead of speaking them. A dull play can spoil good music. It has happened again and again. Bizet's music was good but the stories he chose did not seem to interest people. So he had a hard time and, cheery as he was, he once said that "music is a splendid art but a sad trade."

To earn a living Bizet had to give lessons in piano playing and do all sorts of musical chores for publishers. But he never lost heart nor felt too sorry for himself. He kept on writing the beautiful music that sang in his brain, even though he had to work night and day to do it.

At last fortune seemed to smile on Bizet. He made a happy choice in a story for an opera. It was the story of Carmen, the Spanish gypsy. His music suited it perfectly. This was an opera which was to make him famous, but he was never to enjoy this fame. Three months after *Carmen* was first given, Bizet died very suddenly, at his home near Paris.

CHILDREN'S GAMES

Bizet wrote a set of twelve little pieces which he called *Children's Games*. He wrote these pieces for two players at the piano—two pairs of hands on the keyboard instead of one. Any piece written especially for two singers or players is called a *duet*.

Later Bizet decided to let other instruments play *Children's Games*. He arranged these piano duets for the orchestra. To arrange a piece for the orchestra means writing special parts for the different kinds of instruments. Or, if an orchestra piece is arranged for the piano, the arranger must see that all the important notes that have been played by a number of instruments are rewritten in such a way that one pair of hands can play them on the piano.

It is rather like what happens in a game. A boy can play ball alone or with another boy, pitching the ball back and forth. But when boys play baseball, they do not want nine pitchers. Baseball takes more players and each player has his own special part.

Each of the pieces in *Children's Games* has two names. First there is a name which tells its music pattern—what kind of a piece it is. Then there is the name of the game Bizet was thinking about when he wrote the music.

March—Trumpet and Drum

Trumpet and Drum seems name enough for this piece. Of course it would be a march. Whoever heard of a waltz or a cradle song played by trumpet and drum! Marches always make us think of soldiers. Soldiers were among the first to discover that when a number of people are trying to do the same thing, it is much easier if they keep together. One of the things soldiers have to do is walk, sometimes for miles and miles. It was very tiresome when they straggled along like cattle in a field, each going his own way. It seemed much easier when they learned to step together, and it was really pleasant when they stepped to music. So although we may hear marching music in parades, in school, and even in church, we always think of the march as being, first of all, soldier music.

Trumpet and Drum is very soldierly sounding. The drum taps and rolls:

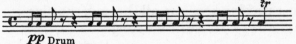

A brave, little tune begins to march:

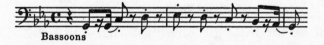

and then the trumpet's clear voice gives the signals:

63

In spite of its military airs, we soon find out that *Trumpet and Drum* is only a play-soldier march for children. Real soldiers would have no room to stretch their legs to such a tune! It is a tune for little legs. Then, too, the instruments sound rather toylike. Pages of the score are just peppered with signs, *p* and *pp* and *ppp*, which say, "soft, softer, softest" to the players.

After a while we hear a pretty little tune:

which has a great many trills and tinkles. It seems to belong to some very fancy marching. The soldiers must be doing a parade drill. The tune goes up and down and round about in all sorts of figures. The trumpeter is a busy fellow. His cheeks are almost bursting with the many signals he has to blow. But he keeps bravely at it, and so does the drummer, to the end of the drill.

Berceuse—The Doll's Cradle Song

The French word for lullaby is *berceuse*. This music pictures a little girl rocking her doll to sleep. We can feel the motion of the cradle—rockaby, rockaby:

This gentle rocking keeps up all through the piece.

As the cradle rocks, we hear a song:

It must be the little girl singing to her doll baby. The tune sounds as if it were saying, "Now go to sleep, my baby."

Different instruments sing the cradle song, first the violins, then the clarinets, flutes, and oboes in turn, while the rest of the orchestra softly plays just a note here and there.

At the very end the flute whispers the little song tune, and all the instruments join in the last chord. If you could see all the *ppp*s written below those last notes, you might almost expect to see the orchestra men put their fingers to their lips as if to say, "Sssh!! Don't waken this doll baby!"

Impromptu—The Top

This is surely a boy's tune, if ever there was one. It starts off with a single sharp, bright tone, as if the top had touched the pavement with a *ping!* Then we hear a humming and spinning:

and then, above the whirring, a saucy little tune:

It might be the boy whistling as he spins the top. Or it might be the tune of the top itself. You may have seen one of those beautiful big tops, ringed with gay colors, that play little tunes as they spin.

All of a sudden, something happens. The spinning stops and the tune stops. There is a grumbling sort of chord that sounds as if the top had run down and toppled over. Then a to-do among the strings sounds as if they might be winding it up again.

Sure enough, just as at first, *ping!* Down it goes on the pavement. It begins to spin and then to play its tune. It runs down and is rewound a second time, but we do not wait to see it spin.

Before we go on to the next of the *Children's Games*, let's answer the good reader who is wondering about the word "impromptu." It means something done suddenly, without much getting ready. In music, an *impromptu* is a short piece which sounds like a bright idea, rather than something over which the composer had worked. *The Top* certainly sounds like a sudden happy thought, and no doubt Bizet enjoyed it as much as we do!

Duo—Little Husband and Little Wife

If you were to hear this piece without knowing its title, you would think, "What a peaceful, comfortable-sounding tune."

And if you were a specially good listener you might add, "It sounds as if two people were talking." So it does, for Bizet was thinking of two people when he wrote it—a little girl and boy, playing house. "I'll be the lady and you be the man"— you know that game!

From the peacefulness of the music we know that this make-believe husband and wife are happy together. The little wife speaks first:

She must be speaking of something pleasant. The tune would not sound so smooth and beautiful if she were telling her husband how naughty their little boy doll had been that day.

Then we hear the deeper voice of the little man:

He must be agreeing with her, for his tune repeats what she has been saying. Their voices sound so pretty together!

They seem to talk about different things, but every little while one or the other mentions that pleasant thing the little wife told her husband in the beginning. What do you suppose it was?

Scherzo—Wooden Horses

Today's children—and that means you too—are fortunate. You have so many adventures, so many things that girls and boys of long ago never even dreamed of. But yesterday's children had some things you might well envy. They had horses and ponies. A pony is surely one of the dearest of live playthings. There are so few horses in today's street pictures that if it were not for the mounted policemen, many a child would scarcely know what a horse looks like! Children who do not know about horses miss one of the nicest games, playing horse.

The streets of Paris were full of horses when Georges Bizet was a little boy. He must have liked them, or he would not have put Wooden Horses into his *Children's Games*.

In the first few measures of this piece, before the tune

begins, you feel the galloping rhythm:

These galloping notes sound much like hoofbeats and they keep up all through the piece. Above them comes the tune:

If you know about horses and riding, you can feel yourself going up and down in the saddle.

But, as you listen to this music, you may begin to feel that with all their wild galloping these horses aren't getting anywhere. They seem to be going 'round and 'round. And so they should, for these are the wooden horses of a merry-go-round! Surely you know about merry-go-round horses. They don't get anywhere but who cares? They are bright and jolly and so is this little tune, called *scherzo*—a joking, playful piece.

Battledore and Shuttlecock

An old-fashioned game called battledore and shuttlecock gave Bizet the idea for one of his prettiest tunes. This game is something like tennis and is played with a paddle, or battledore, which looks like a small tennis racket. But instead of a ball which can bounce, there is a shuttlecock—a large cork stuck full of feathers. The idea of the game is not to let the shuttlecock touch the ground. The players run to and fro striking it with their little paddles. The feathers help to keep it in the air.

Bizet's *Battledore and Shuttlecock* is so light and fast that you get very little idea of it from this small sample:

67

But it is easy to picture the game when you hear the whole piece. The back-and-forth feeling of the music suggests the players running and making little leaps as they strike with their paddles. And there is a lightness, a sort of up-in-the-air feeling, of the feathered shuttlecock. Old game books call battledore and shuttlecock an *aerial* game, which means "moving in the air." Surely this is an aerial tune!

Galop—The Doll's Ball

Our *Children's Games* end with an old-fashioned dance known as the *galop*. The dolls seem to be having a grand ball. The tune begins:

and away they go, boy dolls in uniforms and dress suits, girl dolls in the sweetest little flower frocks, all smiling and pleased with their ball. Near the end the music is marked *con furia*. No need to run to the dictionary to find what that means. The music tells us. The players are playing "with fury," the dancers are dancing "with fury," and even we listeners are a bit out of breath with all of this fury!

7.

Camille Saint-Saëns

Paris—1835
Algiers—1921

More than a century ago, two worried women looked at a frail little French baby and wondered what in the world to do with it! The baby's father had just died of a dreadful disease and the doctors had said that the tiny son might not live. But these women, the mother and the aunt, made up their minds to fight for the baby's life. Although he was but three months old, they sent him out into the country with a nurse. There, for two years, his sickly body soaked up the fresh air and sunshine, and he came back to Paris laughing and rosy-cheeked.

His "two mothers," as Saint-Saëns lovingly called them, soon found that they had a very unusual child on their hands. Camille's busy little brain gave them no peace. He was curious about everything, and particularly about the sounds he heard. At two, he was imitating the tones of bells, striking clocks, creaking doors, and other household noises, and trying to find out just how they were made. He would sit on a little stool beside the fireplace, perfectly fascinated by the tune of the boiling teakettle. At two and a half, he would amuse himself at the piano. He did not pound a fist full of notes as most youngsters do. He carefully pressed down one key at a time, listening and waiting until one sound had completely died away before making another. Almost before they knew it, he could call those notes by name. This was no doubt the beginning of that marvelous memory for sounds which later distinguished Saint-Saëns, the composer.

When Camille was four years old, he was making little waltzes of his own. At five, he could play Mozart's music very well. At ten, he gave a public concert with an orchestra, playing a whole program of difficult music from memory!

A spiteful woman said to Mme. Saint-Saëns, "If your boy

is allowed to play Beethoven at ten, whose music will there be left for him to play at twenty?"

"Oh," replied the mother calmly, "he will be playing his own music then!" She was a true prophet, for, by the time he was twenty, Saint-Saëns' first symphony had not only been played by a Paris orchestra, but praised by the celebrated composers, Gounod and Berlioz.

Camille's mother and aunt were too wise to let him grow up a queer, one-sided genius. There were to be no child prodigy concert tours such as had sapped the strength of little Wolfgang Mozart and turned the head of many another clever youngster. Camille was sent to school where he did just as much Latin and geometry as any other boy, and did it well, too.

At eighteen Saint-Saëns was holding his first paid position, as organist in a Parish church. From that time on, his life story is the record of a brilliant and remarkable career. Paris was fairly humming with musical activities, and Saint-Saëns seems to have been part of them all. He gave concerts, wrote a great deal of music of all kinds, and played the organ in the famous Church of the Madeleine. He also spent much time and thought in helping young artists and composers and in trying to teach French audiences to enjoy good music.

He was always a staunch patriot. In the War of 1870 he did his share of soldiering. And in World War I, although he was past eighty, this wonderful old man wrote patriotic pieces and even played in concerts, to earn money for war funds.

With all his work, Saint-Saëns always found time for fun. As a young fellow he was famous at parties for the clever way he acted the part of some famous person, like a well-known woman opera star! And later, in such lovely musical jokes as his *Carnival of the Animals,* and in his delightful sketches, and a little play, "Writer's Cramp," he showed himself a jolly, well-balanced man. No one could accuse Saint-Saëns of having a freakish "artistic temperament."

There were, of course, sorry chapters in Saint-Saëns' life. The War of 1870 took from him several of his dearest friends. And the red days of terror, when Paris trembled under the rule of the merciless Commune, left deep scars on his sensitive nature. The greatest grief of all was the loss of his two little sons. The eldest, a dear little three-year-old, fell from a fourth floor window and was killed. A few weeks later the baby died.

Saint-Saëns had a marvelous collection of friends, among them the most famous artists, musicians, and literary men of the day, and even kings and queens. And no wonder! Here was a talented musician, with beauty at his finger tips, who was an interesting, amusing, and thoroughly nice man as well! One of the things for which his close friends admired him most was his loving thought and care of his mother.

As a composer Saint-Saëns was, above all else, *orderly*. In his music every note and phrase is clear and in its place. He had little patience with some of the young moderns in whose music, as he said, the instruments of the orchestra "run in all directions like poisoned rats." He loved a pretty tune, and he was a wizard with rhythms. Saint-Saëns was equally clever at writing *pattern music,* which pleases us with its lovely designs, and *story and picture music,* which suggests ideas.

In his later life, Saint-Saëns became a great traveler. He went adventuring all over the map and made two trips to the United States. Algiers was his favorite stopping place. Its glimpses of the Orient, its sunny days and beautiful night skies, in which he could study his beloved stars, satisfied many sides of this artist's nature. We find a great many pictures of Algiers in his music. And it was there, at the age of eighty-six, that this man who began life as a frail French baby finished the labors of a musical giant.

THE CARNIVAL OF THE ANIMALS

There are a great many amusing stories, poems, and pictures in the world. It seems easy to make jokes with words and lines. The storyteller has only to begin his, "Once upon a time there were three fat little pigs," and every listening child begins to smile. Or the artist has only to make a few clever strokes with his crayon and there they are—piggy faces and curly tails, droll as life! But it is not so easy for music to be funny.

No matter what he wants to suggest, the composer must stick to his business of making music. He must always remember that music is beautiful tones made into pleasing patterns. Music cannot really tell a story or paint a picture to make us laugh. It can only give us the *feeling* of funny things. But sometimes those funny feelings make us laugh more than any words or lines!

The Carnival of the Animals is one of the few really funny pieces of music. Half the fun is in the music itself—the clever way the notes suggest the animals. Let's not miss anything when we listen to this music. Let's laugh at these animals and then let's take a peep behind the scenes, to see how composer Saint-Saëns made these funny things—and laugh again!

It was carnival time in Paris. This carnival is the last big frolic before the season of Lent, when people are supposed to live quietly and think of more serious things. Carnival time is a very gay time. Everybody seems to be trying to crowd weeks of fun into a few hours. The streets swarm with merrymakers in masks and queer costumes, singing, dancing, and playing all sorts of pranks. The theaters and music halls, too, are filled with holiday crowds.

Saint-Saëns wanted to write a surprise piece for one of the carnival concerts. It must, of course, be merry music, funny if possible. Why not an animal carnival to amuse these human carnival celebrators? It was a grand idea. For animals are both beautiful and amusing, as this music should be.

Saint-Saëns was just the person to write about animals, for he had always loved them. He really tried to know them and often went to the zoological gardens to watch them. He had many animal friends, not only his own pets but other people's. Once he wrote an essay called "The Friend of Animals," in which he tells of clever things he had seen them do. Animals, he thought, were not so dumb, even if they couldn't speak— not nearly so dumb as some people who talk a lot! And as he thought about some of the stupid people he knew, especially some stupid musicians there in Paris, he couldn't resist having fun with them. So he put them right into the animal's carnival!

The piece was not finished in time for the carnival concert. Later it was played at a private concert. Saint-Saëns himself played one of the piano parts. Everyone was delighted with *The Carnival of the Animals*. The composer was urged to play it again and to let it be published. But Saint-Saëns feared that his fun-making might hurt someone's feelings. So during his lifetime he would never let this music be played publicly or printed.

After his death they found a paragraph in his will giving permission to publish *The Carnival of the Animals*. So, you see, this music is a legacy—that means a gift from someone who is gone. Saint-Saëns left it to be enjoyed by all of us.

Introduction

The introduction to *The Carnival of the Animals* is very short—just a sign that says, "This way to the animals." We scarcely need a printed sign when we are going to a real zoo. Our ears usually tell us where we are, and so they do in this music. Just listen! What a medley of roars, brays, clucks, and squawks! The nearer we come, the louder it sounds. Then a sharp chord seems to shout, "Quiet!" There is a pause—

Royal March of the Lion

Then a grand flourish:

Someone very important must be coming! Here he is, the King of the Beasts, the lion:

And isn't he royal! His tune sounds a bit queer and rough, but remember he comes from the African jungle. No pretty parlor pieces for him!

He has a grand voice and, as he passes, he salutes us:

The pianos are bold enough to answer:

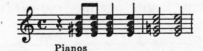

73

There are fierce, short growls:

Then a last mighty roar:

and His Royal Highness disappears.

But did you notice that, uncivilized as he is, the lion roars in tune? Saint-Saëns is not letting even the King of Beasts spoil his music.

Hens and Cocks

Can it be hens and cocks, crowding right in on the heels of His Majesty? What a comedown! Hear those hens cackling:

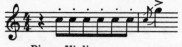

one after another. Now my lords, the cocks, enter, three of them, one after another:

How proudly they step along, raising their yellow legs like little dancing masters and arching their necks. Cocks always act as if they thought the whole barnyard was watching and admiring them. Attention, please—"Cock-a-doodle-do!"

Isn't the clarinet cocky and funny?

Then the hens begin again—*"cut-cut-cut-cut-cut-cut-ca-dawcut"*:

74

all foolish and excited, until the pianos can't stand their racket and cut them right off! You will notice that the pianos seem to be master of ceremonies. Saint-Saëns himself played the first piano part when *The Carnival of the Animals* was first played.

Hémiones—Fleet-footed Animals

Hémiones is a French word that means wild donkeys or wild Tartar horses such as gallop over the plains of Central Asia. Whatever they are, they certainly are fleet-footed! Back and forth and up and down they race:

But their furious speed doesn't seem to get them anywhere. Silly things! Have you ever known people who were always racing about, always in a hurry and seeming to be so busy, yet had little to show for all their fuss? Saint-Saëns knew some, particularly some fashionable pianists who were trying to fool Paris audiences. They made a great show, racing their fingers up and down the keyboard, but they made very little real music. Saint-Saëns' friends knew that he was thinking of these scampering pianists when he wrote *Hémiones*.

Turtles

There is certainly nothing frisky about this procession of dull, old turtles:

What a sluggish, dragging tune, you think. Not at all! The joke is that this is really a very bright, fast tune! Saint-Saëns borrowed it from the ballet music of a very popular opera. Imagine how amazed people were to hear it creeping along at turtle tempo! And imagine how they laughed!

Notice how the tune seems to carry the accompaniment all

75

piled on its back:

That's rather "turtlish" too!

There are two places where it sounds like wrong notes. The chords are messy—just such muddy harmonies as might be expected of turtles. And how the accompaniment seems to push at the tune! It really is too clever of Saint-Saëns to use a slow motion for the tune:

and a faster one for the accompaniment:

It gives a feeling of drag and push, as if someone were prodding the turtles with a stick.

But you cannot hurry these fellows. By the time the tune reaches the last few measures, you feel that you must help push these notes into their chords or they will never get there!

The Elephant

Here is the elephant masquerading as a dancer, a toe dancer at that! What a sight he is in his short, frilly skirts, kicking and twirling and trying to be airy:

And if his tune isn't from Berlioz's famous *Dance of the Sylphs!*

There is also a snatch of Mendelssohn's fairy scherzo from the Midsummer Night's Dream music:

Double Bass

Sylph and fairy dances trodden by an elephant! And played by the *double bass*—the elephant of the orchestra! What could be more ridiculous!

If there is a prize for the most foolish fellow at the animals' carnival, surely the elephant deserves it!

Kangaroos

Such hopping:

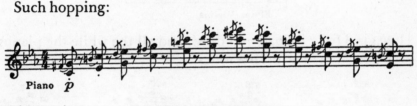

Piano *p*

and jumping:

Piano *pp*

can only belong to those champion long-jumpers, the kangaroos. How plainly you can feel the difference between the hopping and the jumping. And how like magic it is, that a few little black marks on a page can give these feelings!

There are many musical tricks in this kangaroo music to interest the child who likes to make discoveries and to know the reasons why. But it isn't just trick music. There is a nice little tune underneath all the bouncing. And those long jumps land on some very pretty chords.

Aquarium

If it were not for aquariums most of us would have no chance to enjoy the beauty of fish. In the real ponds and streams we can only catch a glimpse of these swift, shy creatures. The most beautiful thing about a fish is its motion. In the aquarium we can watch this beautiful, noiseless motion. We like to follow the ever-changing pattern of darts and curves, of delicate curling fins and tails. The water moves too, gently rippling and swaying. Water plants, like soft green feathers, wave back and forth. And sometimes, in the larger aquariums, slow starfish and jewel-eyed crabs crawl about on the white sandy bottom.

Saint-Saëns has caught all this beautiful movement in his music. Flutes, muted violins, and the bell-like celesta play the melody:

How gracefully it floats and dips! And all the while the pianos are suggesting the rippling water:

Notice how many more notes it takes to ripple than to float.

There is the suggestion of color in this picture. You think of the green of water plants, the pink and ivory tints of shells and sand, and then of all the rainbow colors that flash from glistening fish scales and sparkling water. There is a scale made of half tones—playing a scale on the piano, using all the

78

black and white keys, gives an idea of it. This is called the *chromatic scale,* or colored scale. Saint-Saëns uses it to make us think of color.

Near the end of the piece there is a place where it sounds as if little bubbles came foaming up:

Then, with a last glimpse of the murmuring water, we lose sight of the aquarium.

Long-eared Persons

These gentlemen with the long ears need no introduction. Everyone knows who they are:

And don't you get a kicking feeling as you listen to their hee-hawing? Surely it is not just imagination that makes us see those hind-leg gestures with which long-eared persons often accompany their conversation. To think of respectable fiddles behaving like this!

The Cuckoo in the Deep Woods

Have you ever gone into a deep wood? Do you remember how sweet it smelled? Perhaps you saw a carpet of brown leaves and moss embroidered with ferns and tiny white flowers or scarlet berries—a carpet over which timid forest folk went scampering on their errands.

Saint-Saëns pictures just such a deep, quiet wood in this music. There is a procession of rather solemn chords:

which makes you think of great shadowy trees. It is all so still. Even the breeze is hushed. Suddenly the silence is broken by a clear call, "cuckoo!":

You cannot see him. He is only a voice. He has no real song, but just keeps repeating his name on the same two tones.

You may think that it was easy to write this cuckoo call of just two tones. But try any other two tones with this forest music and you will soon see that it took a clever musician to put the cuckoo in the deep woods. This is one of the really beautiful pieces in *The Carnival of the Animals*. It is not funny, and a good listener does not laugh.

Aviary

More birds, but how different from the shy little cuckoo! These birds live in an aviary—a cage so large that it is almost like a piece of the out-of-doors.

This is not quiet music. It is light and delicate, but full of a ceaseless commotion. One little bird holds the center of the stage with his fancy, fluting song:

But the others pay no attention to him. They are far too busy.

Such a fluttering of wings:

and darting to and fro. Such trilling:

and whistling:

It is plain to be seen that these birds are quite used to being watched and admired. They sound as if they like this aviary.

80

Pianists

Here are some very surprising animals called pianists. The wildest variety wear long-tailed coats and have manes of moppy hair. They have strange habits. They exercise their fingers, like this:

and every once in a while they make a fearful bang like this:

They keep this up for hours, and they do it in every key! It is bad enough when they play the right notes, but when they fumble and play wrong ones, as these fellows do, the neighbors almost go mad. That growly scolding in the strings:

might be one of those angry neighbors! Or do you suppose these fierce pianists growl?

Saint-Saëns himself was a pianist—a very famous one. So, you see, he knew what he was about when he put fumbling, pounding pianists in a cage!

Fossils

Before the pianists have finished their last chord, an even stranger group breaks in. It is the fossils. Fossils are the remains of plants and animals that have been buried in the earth for hundreds of years. Sometimes they have turned to stone. Sometimes they are merely prints—hoofmarks or the pattern of a fern leaf clearly marked in what once was clay. The word "fossil" means dug up.

Fossils are very important in the study of the earth's history.

81

They are interesting, too, but most of us would rather see a living plant or animal than a "has been." Saint-Saëns was a very live person and had very little patience with any sort of "has been." He knew some tunes that had been played and sung until it seemed to him that there was no life left in them. They were *fossils!* So, while he was making fun of blundering pianists, why not make fun of these fossil tunes!

He began by digging up one of his own, the famous *Dance of Death:*

played by the bony xylophone.

Then he shows traces of four other "has been" tunes—a sentimental song, an air from a well-known opera, and two old folk songs. Every child knows this one:

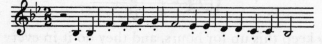

But his own tune seems to bore him most. He comes back to it and pounds it out as though it were a stone tune with no feeling at all!

The Swan

Last comes *The Swan,* one of the loveliest of all tone pictures. We see a little lake:

Notice how the first piano makes the ripples, while the second marks that slow swaying which is to be the rhythm of the piece.

Then, on the smooth tones of the cello, the swan glides by:

Cello

Like a queen she moves along. No inquisitive frog or spying water-bug would dare ask her where she is going. The beautiful, floating melody tells us that she is not going anywhere. What has she to do with muddy banks! She belongs to a dream world of drifting clouds and swaying water lilies. We watch her sail out of sight beyond the willow tree, and for a moment we wonder—was it real or were we too in a dream world?

Finale

The animals' carnival is over. We get the same zoo-like medley of voices as in the beginning, and we think we have heard the last of these amusing creatures. But no. The flute and piccolo begin to whistle a jaunty little tune:

Piccolo Flute

Back they all come prancing, like actors making their bows in front of the curtain when the show is over.

The swan does not come back, she is much too dignified. And the turtles do not get there, they are probably too slow. But you will recognize most of the others, the wild donkeys, cocks and hens, and kangaroos. And, of course, the gentlemen with the long ears, who manage to get the last word—and they would!

Do you wonder that people begged Saint-Saëns to play this merry music? And aren't you glad that he finally let it be published so that we can all enjoy the musical jokes?

8

Maurice Ravel

Ciboure—1875
Paris—1937

Maurice Ravel was born in the beautiful French mountains not far from the Spanish border. When he was still a baby, he was taken to Paris to live. As a child, he loved music and wanted to find out all he could about it. So he learned to play the piano, and later he learned about the many instruments of the orchestra and what they could do. He was interested in composing and, before he was twenty, began to write music.

It was strange music, full of all sorts of curious ideas. Ravel's teachers hardly knew what to say about it, because it was so different from the music in their study books. But they found this strange music interesting, and they respected the boy because he was so much in earnest about it.

Ravel had always loved the music of ancient days. Many of his pieces are made after the old quaint patterns. He also loved to make story and picture music. He could compose his tunes so cleverly that when we hear them we too begin to think of stories and pictures. Nearly always we seem to make the very stories Ravel meant us to make. It really is a kind of magic!

So Ravel lived in Paris, writing his strange music. Sometimes he made pieces for the piano, sometimes for orchestra or for small groups of strings, and sometimes he made songs.

Then World War I came. Like all people who love beautiful things, Ravel dreaded the thought of all the blood and pain and ugliness of war. He was not a large man with a great strong body. He might easily have said, "I would not make a good soldier anyway. Let the husky fellows do the fighting. I'll save myself to make music which the world certainly needs." But Ravel had too big and brave a heart for such talk. When his country needed men he joined the colors.

He drove a truck, and right up to the front lines, too. It was hard work and dangerous. But Ravel kept at it until his body gave out. For a long time he could not work at all, not even at his music.

When he grew better he went to live in a village not far from Paris. There in a little "doll's house," perched on the side of a steep hill, he worked away at his music and entertained his friends. He was so witty that people who knew him enjoyed his talk almost as much as his music. Ravel loved children and animals. He could imitate the calls of birds and animals quite wonderfully. Cats were his special delight and amusement. He once shared his house with a whole family of pussies. Someone said, "He not only understood cats—he could talk their language."

Ravel often traveled about giving concerts and directing orchestras when they were playing his music. He gave many concerts in the United States.

In the winter of 1937, Maurice Ravel died in a hospital in Paris and the musical world lost one of the most delightful composers of the twentieth century.

The Mother Goose Suite

All American children know and love their Mother Goose—those jolly jingles about Jack Horner, Humpty Dumpty, Little Bopeep, and the rest. French children love their Mother Goose, too. But their Mother Goose is not the same as ours. It is a set of old fairy tales, some of which we also know.

When Ravel wanted to make a set of little story tunes he could think of nothing nicer than to tell some of these old fairy tales. He called them *Ma Mere l'Oye*, which is the French way of saying Mother Goose. He first wrote this set of pieces to be played on the piano. Then he thought they would be even more fun when played by the instruments of the orchestra. So he rewrote *The Mother Goose Suite* for the orchestra. Sometimes dancers take the parts of these fairy-tale characters and act out the stories while the music plays. Then we call it a *ballet*.

Ravel liked stories and story music and all childish things. He must have had a good time making his Mother Goose music. But he worked hard at these childish pieces and put his very best ideas into them. Ravel knew that children can be very particular about the music they hear. He also knew that grown people would be constantly borrowing these pieces for their own concerts. For here's a secret. *No clever person ever grows up completely!*

Just see if you can't catch your own father smiling over your toys sometime. You will surely catch your teacher enjoying these very little tunes!

The Mother Goose Suite is a charming present to all music-loving children. It is a present to *you*. As you listen to it, see if you don't agree that every note is exactly in its right place!

Pavane of the Sleeping Beauty

You know the story of "The Sleeping Beauty," don't you? How once upon a time a young prince, hunting in the forest, came upon a place where the trees stood so close together and the vines and bushes made such a thick mat that even a rabbit might snag his coat if he tried to go through. Above the tree-tops just the tip of a castle tower could be seen.

"What a strange place!" said the Prince. "It looks as if it had been asleep for a hundred years!"

"And so it has, Your Highness, if all the tales be true," said one of the Prince's followers.

"Tales? What tales?" asked the Prince. "Speak up, tell us!"

"Why, Your Highness," answered the man, "I've often heard my grandfather say that when he was but a boy his grandfather told him that in yonder castle a princess lies in a magic sleep. She must sleep for a hundred years!"

"Oh, how nice!" squeaked a lazy little page.

"Don't interrupt, boy!" said the Prince sternly.

"And when the hundred years are up," continued the story teller, "a king's son is to awaken her. They say she is very beautiful!"

"How exciting!" cried the Prince. "You say your grandfather's father told him—why the hundred years must be about over! I'm a king's son! And I'm just the fellow for such an adventure! I think I'll take a look at the lady!" And he began to part the heavy bushes.

His followers begged him not to go near the enchanted castle. Strange mishaps can occur to those who meddle with magic. But the Prince only laughed at their fears. He pushed into the thicket, which closed behind him, and forced his way

86

through to the castle. How still it was! Not a leaf stirred, not a flower nodded, not a bird note could be heard, the very clouds hung motionless above him. As he crossed the marble courtyard, the Prince saw two soldiers guarding the door. He listened for their challenge, "Who goes there!" But there was not a sound. Stiff and straight, with their muskets over their shoulders, the guards stood—*fast asleep!*

The Prince tiptoed past the sleeping guards, entered the castle, and peeped into the rooms. There seemed to be plenty of people about. There were the ladies in waiting with their fans, and the gentlemen of the court with their snuff boxes and their pretty manners, some standing, some sitting, but all—*fast asleep!* There were the court musicians with their horns to their lips and their fiddle bows raised, but all—*fast asleep!*

In the kitchen the cook, with a huge spoon in his hand, bent over his soup pot—*snoring!* The maid, plucking a goose for dinner, sat with her fingers full of feathers and her nose twisted just ready to sneeze but—*snoring!* Why even the horses in the stalls, the great hunting dogs, the goldfish in the pool, and the pigeons on the roof were all—*fast asleep!*

At last the Prince came to a beautiful room in the middle of which stood a bed all hung with blue and silver embroideries. And there, with her golden curls gleaming on the satin pillow and her sweet lips curved in a smile, lay the loveliest little princess—*fast asleep!*

The Prince rubbed his eyes. Was this all a dream? Had he too fallen asleep? Then he felt his heart turn one big somersault. My goodness! How he loved her! More than anything in the world he wanted to see the eyes hidden beneath those rose petal eyelids. He must waken her. But how?

Then the Prince did exactly the right thing. He fell on his knees beside the bed and gently kissed the hand of the Sleeping Beauty.

Slowly the lovely eyes opened. Cornflower blue they were, and shiny as stars. And, will you believe me, they were not at all startled at sight of a strange young man kneeling there. The Princess must have been dreaming about her Prince all that long while! For as soon as she saw him she said, in a voice that sounded like silver bells, "It is you, my Prince!"

Then all of the court wakened. The horses shook themselves

and neighed, the hounds sprang up and wagged their tails, the pigeons on the roof drew their heads from under their wings. The kitchen fire leapt up and cooked the meat, the cook gave the soup a stir and the kitchen boy such a box on the ears that he roared out, and the maid sneezed and went on plucking the goose!

How fresh they all felt and no wonder! And how hungry! And how happy they all were, in spite of the fact that their clothes were a hundred years behind the styles!

The Prince married the Princess that very same evening. It was a grand wedding! Fairies came with presents of good wishes and, they say, there never was a happier pair than Prince Charming and his Sleeping Beauty.

Sleeping Beauty lived in the days when there was time to do almost everything graciously. Each hour in the day of a princess—her walks in the park, her lessons, her meals, and even her dressing and undressing—was marked with much ceremony.

It was indeed a great event when the fairy wand touched the Princess, at the beginning of our story, and she began to grow drowsy with the magic sleep. The court musicians played soft music and all the courtiers and the ladies in waiting began to dance. It was not the lively dancing we know, the dancing of a merry party. It was a slow and stately dance with which the people of long ago used to celebrate solemn occasions. This dance came from Italy and is called a *pavane*, the Italian word for "peacock," a proud, gorgeous, and solemn bird.

The flute plays this little tune:

pp

It is the tune of the dream which, like a chiffon curtain, was slowly falling about the little Princess, shutting out all the sights and sounds of the wide-awake world.

Underneath the dream runs another tune:

in which we can hear the dancers stepping about softly, not to disturb the sleeping princess.

All the instruments play so gently. The horns wear their mutes. The strings are barely touched with the fingers, and the harps are a mere shimmer of sound.

Surely this is the nodding music of sleep! Close your eyes and let it sway you, just the least little bit. Don't you begin to have a sort of "sorry to wake up" feeling?

Hop o' My Thumb

Once upon a time there was a woodcutter and his wife who had seven little boys. The youngest was so very tiny when he was born that someone jokingly said, "Why, he is no bigger than my thumb!" And so it was that the child came by the queer nickname "Little Thumb," or "Hop o' My Thumb."

Now the woodcutter was very poor. His master would not pay him his wages, his cow died, his garden dried up, and everything seemed to go wrong. At last there came a day when there was not a penny in the purse, nor a pint of meal for the pot. And seven little boys held up their little bowls and begged for supper!

After the children had gone to bed, the woodcutter and his wife sat talking. "What shall we do?" cried the mother. "Are we to see our children die of hunger before our very eyes?"

"No, no," sighed the father, "that I could never bear. I would rather take them out and lose them in the forest than sit here and watch them starve."

The poor mother wept bitterly at such a plan, but she could think of nothing else to do. She kissed the little fellows as they lay sleeping. "Oh, my poor children," she sobbed, "little do you know what tomorrow will bring to you!"

But Hop o' My Thumb knew. He had been awake and had heard what his father had said. As soon as his parents were abed, he crept out of the house and filled his pockets with small white stones. Hop o' My Thumb had a plan too!

The next morning the woodcutter's family went into the forest as usual. The father led the children into a deep thicket and told them to pick up sticks for the fire. While they were busy with this, he slipped away and left them.

When the sticks were all piled in neat little bundles, the boys called to their father to come and see what they had

89

done. They called again and again, but there was no answer save the lonesome hoot of an owl.

"Where can Father have gone?" cried Peter.

"He never left us before!" said Philip.

"And oh, it is getting so dark," sobbed Jaimie.

"And I hear the wolves, I'm afraid," wailed Henry.

"Don't cry! Don't cry!" piped Hop o' My Thumb. "Just come with me and I'll take you home."

"You'll take us home!" chorused his brothers in surprise.

"You're so little you don't know what you're talking about!" said Peter, the oldest.

"Just the same, I'm going with Hop," said Jaimie. "His head may not be big but it's good and full!"

So they followed their tiny brother and found that he had dropped little stones all along, through the forest, to mark the way. And sure enough, presently the pebbly trail brought them right to their father's door.

The woodcutter and his wife were sitting at supper when the children got home. That very evening the woodcutter's master had paid his debt and they had been able to buy something to eat. They were glad to see the little boys and fed them well as long as the food lasted.

But in a few days the cupboard was empty again. Once more they took the children into the forest. This time the father saw to it that Hop o' My Thumb had no pebbles in his pockets. But the child had saved his breakfast crust of bread and, as they went along, he scattered crumbs to mark the path.

The woodcutter left the children, as before. But this time they were not afraid. Hop o' My Thumb again promised to lead them home and they set out cheerily. But alas, he could not find the way, his markers were gone! The birds had eaten every single crumb!

Here the music takes up the story. First it shows us the long path winding through the forest:

In and out, and up and down, the path tune goes. Above it we hear the voices of the children. At first they seem to be singing a little wanderer's song. They try to be cheerful, for although

90

the way is long, didn't Hop lead them out safely before? The forest is so big and the children so little, their tune sounds rather lonesome:

They begin to question: "Oh, Hop, and are you sure this is the right path?"

The tiny boy bravely leads on and they take heart for a moment. The music sounds less forlorn. Then Hop o' My Thumb begins to feel anxious. Where, oh where, are his precious crumbs? Who can have taken them away?

The answer comes from the branches above him. Birds begin to twitter and chirp their thanks for the nice supper of crumbs that kind Hop o' My Thumb had spread for them!

Ravel makes very clever bird music with flutes and violins. This is the way the "cheep, cheep, cheep" looks on paper:

Poor little Hop o' My Thumb! Poor little brothers! It is growing dark. They dare not lie down or the wolves will find them. Their feet are so tired! We hear them sigh as they trudge along:

But there is nothing else they can do. There seems nothing in the whole world but that dreary path stretching out before them!

Did you ever hear such lost-sounding music! But listen carefully to the very last chord. It gives you a hint of what happens next, for though the music ends with the path in the woods, the story goes on. The children finally see a light—as cheerful as that last chord we hear at the close of this music.

Laideronette, Empress of the Pagodas

A queen mother once gave a christening party for her little twin princesses. The fairies were invited to this party—that is, all but one. This fairy was so ill-natured that she was quite apt to be forgotten when pleasant things were going on. The forgotten fairy was so angry that she came to the party anyway and, before the other fairies could stop her, she ran to the cradles where the beautiful babies were sleeping and changed one of them into the ugliest little creature imaginable.

This poor baby was now so very plain looking that none of the usual princess names such as Rosemunde and Isabella seemed to suit her. So they christened her Laideronette, which in French means "Little Ugly Girl."

As she grew older Laideronette felt most unhappy going about the palace with her beautiful twin. For this sister's good looks made her own ugliness all the more striking. So Laideronette went to live by herself in a faraway castle.

Here she had the most amazing adventures, and all because of a hideous green serpent. One day she went for a ride in her pretty, painted boat. The boat upset, and Laideronette would surely have drowned had not the serpent come swimming to her rescue. He took her to the curious kingdom of Pagodia.

She found herself surrounded by a crowd of the queerest little folk. They looked like tiny Chinese idols. Most of them were frightfully ugly.

"We are the Pagodas," they chorused in wee, squeaky voices, "and we are commanded to entertain you. You shall be our empress."

They led her to a splendid palace which was to be her new home. They brought her everything her heart could desire. They also gave her one thing which even as a rich little princess she had never had. That was admiration. For the Pagodas were so ugly themselves that they thought Laideronette was perfectly beautiful! And they were forever telling her so.

In the palace garden was a lovely pool. Here Laideronette used to bathe in the cool of the evening. It was a very grand bath indeed! "She laid aside her robes and entered the bath. At once all the Pagodas began to sing and play. Some had lutes made of walnut shells; others had viols made of almond shells; these were instruments in proportion to their own size."

92

Laideronette lived very happily among the Pagodas. After a while she discovered that the king of Pagodia was the Green Serpent himself. And, what is even more surprising, it turned out that this terrible Green Serpent was not really a serpent at all! He was a handsome prince who had been bewitched by the same wicked fairy that had stolen Laideronette's beauty!

In the end, of course, the Green Serpent got himself changed back into a prince. Laideronette lost her ugliness and became as beautiful as she was meant to be. And even the funny little Pagodas, who it seemed were also under a spell, turned into real people. And they all lived happily together in the beautiful palace.

Ravel has chosen for his music that part of the story where the Empress Laideronette bathed in the pool.

First we hear the Pagodas playing music. Perhaps they are practicing to make their piece quite perfect for the Empress. But what queer sounding music! Just the sort one might expect from droll little Chinese idols. Ravel made these tunes from the notes of the Chinese scale. He used many unusual instruments like the celesta, the playing bells, the xylophone, gong and cymbals, to make it sound like a tiny, fairy orchestra.

The piccolo pipes a merry, jigging tune:

He pipes it so energetically that he sets them all going. Presently their music begins to sound like the "Chopsticks" piece children sometimes play on the piano. Do you suppose Ravel could have had the Pagodas play "Chopsticks" on purpose?

But their practicing is interrupted by a solemn sound. The Empress is approaching. The master of ceremonies beats on the gong, and they all bow so low that their foreheads touch the ground:

Then it sounds as if Laideronette, the Empress, were speaking:

and someone answering her:

Then the Pagodas begin to play the piece they were practicing for her. How hard they try, sawing away on their little nutshell instruments for dear life. They do pretty well too! At least we don't notice any mistakes. And what a grand bang at the end! I do hope the Empress liked the Pagodas' music! Did you?

Beauty and the Beast

Once upon a time a traveler lost his way in a deep wood. The sun went down. It grew bitter cold. The man was tired and very hungry. He tried first one path, then another, but he could not find his way out. Just as he was about to give up in despair, he noticed a strange and beautiful house a little ahead of him. As he came nearer he saw that the house stood in a lovely garden. Although it was mid-winter, flowers were blooming there and birds singing gaily in the sweet, warm air! No living creature was to be seen.

The man went into the house, hoping to find food and a place to rest, and someone to tell him the way home. The house was as deserted as the garden, but in one of the rooms was a table spread with the most delicious-looking food. The man was so very hungry that he sat down and ate a hearty supper. Then he spied a comfortable couch that seemed to be waiting for him. So he stretched his weary bones upon it and fell fast asleep. When he awoke he again searched all through the house, but not a soul could he discover.

"What a strange place!" said the man. "I do not like to go away without thanking my host for my good supper and my good bed!"

He went into the garden again. On both sides of the path grew the most beautiful roses the man had ever seen growing.

"How my daughter, Beauty, would love these roses!" said the man. "I shall take one home to her. Surely one rose will not be missed among so many."

But just as he started to pick the rose, a terrible beast appeared and bellowed in a most terrible voice, "What do you mean by picking my roses? For this you shall pay with your life!"

The man hastened to beg the Beast's pardon. He said he had meant no harm. He had wanted only to take one rose to his daughter who loved flowers so dearly. The Beast replied that all that made no difference to him. He was most particular about his roses and whoever touched them must be punished.

"Go on home," he growled. "Take the rose to your daughter. But at the end of one month either one of your daughters must come to live in my house or you must die."

The poor man went sorrowfully home and told his story.

"Well, Father," said Beauty, "since you got into all this trouble through picking a rose for me, I must be the one to go to the Beast's house."

So, at the end of the month. Beauty said good-by to her brothers and sisters and set out for the Beast's house. It was really very brave of her. For although the Beast's house was a wonderful place, the Beast himself was too terrible for words!

All day long Beauty had everything a girl could dream of to make her happy. But every evening after supper the Beast would come shuffling in and ask in his terrible voice, "Beauty, will you marry me?"

Beauty would always answer, as politely as she could, of course, "No, thank you, Beast."

Every night Beauty would dream of a charming prince who begged her to rescue him from a cruel spell that bound him. The prince also urged her not to think too much about the way people looked. He said that a lot of people looked much worse than they really were—all of which is solemn truth! Beauty could not understand what it all meant. But after a while this prince of her dreams seemed very real to her. So real that she loved him!

As the days went by, Beauty found that she really didn't mind the old Beast so much. He couldn't help his beastly looks and he certainly was kind and tried to give her a good time. He even sent Beauty off for a visit with her family, with the promise that she would come back to him in two months' time. But Beauty had such a good time visiting that she was late in coming back to the Beast's house. When she did return, she found the poor fellow lying under a rosebush all but dead. The doctor said he was suffering from a bad case of broken promises. It is a terrible disease. Even beasts curl up and die of it!

"Oh," cried Beauty, "this is all my fault! I am so sorry!"

Her pity seemed like magic medicine. The Beast felt better at once. He was soon able to get up and waddle off.

That evening after supper he came to Beauty's parlor to ask his usual question. A little bird, who was eavesdropping on the window sill, reports this conversation:

Beauty: *(Still feeling sorry)* "When I think of your kind heart, Beast, you don't seem quite so ugly to me."

Beast: *(Sighing)* "Yes, lady, it is true, I've a kind heart, but still I am a monster."

Beauty: *(Still feeling sorry)* "Well, there are many men who are worse monsters than you!"

Beast: *(Gratefully)* "How kind you are! If I were clever I should pay you a fine compliment by way of thanks, but I'm only a Beast! . . . Beauty—will you be my wife?"

Beauty: *(Politely)* "No, thank you, Beast!"

Beast: *(With a sigh that almost split his hide)* "Then I might as well die. But I shall die happy because I have had the joy of seeing you once more, my Beauty!"

Now when the Beast mentioned dying, something happened to Beauty's heart. She knew that she could never be happy without the Beast.

Beauty: *(Eagerly)* "No, no, dear Beast, you must not die! Live, and I will marry you!"

And with that, the Beast disappeared and in his place stood the charming prince of her dreams!

And I'm glad to say that even the little bird that tells things had better manners than to keep on listening and looking at what happened next! But we all know that Beauty and her Prince lived happily ever afterward.

In the music we hear Beauty and the Beast talking together.

Beauty speaks first, in the sweet-speaking voice of the clarinet:

One can tell that she has very pretty manners. She is saying the pleasantest things she can think of to comfort the poor Beast.

Then the Beast speaks:

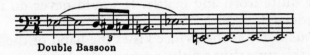

Double Bassoon

Did you ever hear a more horrific voice? No wonder Beauty is alarmed. Even though she is quite used to him and a little fond of him, she can't help thinking, "Oh no! Oh no!" at the idea of marrying him. The violins seem to be crying, "Oh no! Oh no!" under their breath!

The conversation goes on. We can hear them both talking. The Beast pleads with Beauty, his voice grows louder and more eager. When he mentions dying, Beauty's no's are even wilder than before!

Then the harp makes magic. And lo and behold, the Beast disappears! We can hear his thin little beastly ghost voice floating away on soft, high violin tones:

And as it fades it changes into the voice of the Prince!

We hear Beauty answering him.

The music closes with two ideas. One is just a faint memory of how awful the Beast was. The other is the joy of Beauty and her Prince, in the end, told by a last lovely chord of happiness.

The Fairy Garden

The music of *The Fairy Garden* belongs to the story of "The Sleeping Beauty." Ravel began his Mother Goose Suite with the dreamy dance to which the little Princess fell asleep. And since the end of all sleeping is the awakening, it is quite proper that he should end the suite with the awakening of the Sleeping Beauty.

You will remember that the Princess, her court, and even her garden have been asleep for a hundred years. Their dreams must be quite worn and brittle. It would never do to waken them rudely!

So as tenderly as the Prince kisses the hand of the Sleeping Beauty, this tune slips gently in among the dreams:

The Princess stirs in her sleep. Outside in the enchanted garden a little breeze stirs too. A butterfly unfolds his yellow wings. A poplar leaf takes a twirl or two. A goldfish yawns and blows a bubble in the sleepy face of the pond. A daisy opens one eye. Ssh!! They are awakening!

The music sounds nearer. You can feel the sun rising in it. The dainty celesta and the harp begin to glitter and sparkle. The bluebells ring and the trumpet flowers blow a fanfare to announce to all the world that it is morning, and the Sleeping Beauty is awake!

9.

Gabriel Pierné

Metz—1863
Morlaix—1937

Somewhere on your way up from kindergarten you must
have met Robert Louis Stevenson. You may have heard some
of his verses before you started to school, for they are the kind
of verses even very little children know and love. Mr. Stevenson was a grown man when he wrote *A Child's Garden of
Verses,* but as you read them you feel that it is a little boy
speaking. Robert Schumann had the same gift of showing us
his little-boy self in the music of his *Scenes from Childhood.*
It is as if a child had borrowed a man's knowledge, as he might
have borrowed a pencil, just long enough to write down his
own nice child-thoughts.

Here is another man, the French composer Gabriel Pierné,
who writes in much the same delightful way. The city in which
Pierné was born lies so near the German border that, when
the War of 1870 broke out between France and Germany, the
Pierné family moved to Paris. It was a lucky move for seven-
year-old Gabriel, for in Paris there were much better chances
for music lessons and for hearing good music. When he was
eight, the boy entered the Paris Conservatory. He must have
been a very good pupil, for he was accepted by two of the
school's most famous teachers, Massenet and César Franck,
and he carried off many of the school prizes. Young Gabriel
was already trying to write pieces of his own and at twelve had
composed a pretty serenade.

Pierné spent most of his life in Paris. For many years he was
the chief conductor of a celebrated series known as the Colonne
Concerts. He composed music for orchestra and chorus, also
theater music and some delightful ballets.

The books about musicians tell very little about Gabriel
Pierné. But there are other ways of knowing this man. Look-

99

ing at his picture you would feel sure that those fine eyes had seen goodness and beauty. Something else is told by the titles of his pieces—*St. Francis of Assisi,* beautiful music for orchestra with choruses of children, animals and birds; *The Children of Bethlehem, The Children's Crusade,* and *An Album for My Little Friends.* Surely Pierné must have loved children or he wouldn't have put them into his music. As we listen to his music, we would like to have been among those little friends. And we can't help wondering whether Pierné had children of his own. Or did he just write the music of the little Gabriel Pierné he used to be?

Entrance of the Little Fauns—CYDALISE AND THE SATYR

In 1914, just before war cast its terrible shadow over the happiness of the world, Gabriel Pierné finished the music for a jolly ballet called *Cydalise and the Satyr.* The French people have always been fond of stories told by music and dancing and they are very clever at telling them. But in 1914 Paris had no ears for light-hearted music and no feet for dancing. Drums and the tramp of marching men drowned out all pleasant sounds. So for years Pierné's music lay waiting for the noise of guns to die away so that the pipes of fauns could be heard.

The story of this ballet is taken from a curious book called *The Letters of a Satyr,* though I doubt that any satyr could either read or write a letter! The ancient Greeks and Romans had three kinds of gods, those of the heavens, those of the earth, and those of the underworld. Among the earth gods was a strange tribe of wild creatures, part fairy, part animal, who lived in the woods and streams. Their chief was Pan, god of the woods and patron of flocks and shepherds. In his train were wood nymphs, water nymphs and mountain nymphs, lady fairies of surprising beauty. There were also satyrs and fauns, queer snub-nosed fellows with ears, legs, and tails like those of a goat. Dancing seems to have been the main business of satyrs and fauns. Like their master, Pan, they were famous musicians and played such wonderful tunes on their reed pipes that they enchanted simple sheep and the weaker-witted woodfolk. Shepherds, hearing this strange fairy music as they passed some lonely spot, would run for dear life lest their legs go to dancing against their will!

The little fauns, even though they were fairyfolk, went to

100

school. They had to learn to be good musicians. Now, if you can be very quiet and very make-believing, this music will show you the little fauns.

Here we are in a French forest before sunrise. Century-old trees tower above us. A worn carpet of moss, leaf-mold, and creeping plants is soft under our feet. How strange things look in this early morning twilight! It is a picture done in tones of gray—gray tree trunks, gray veils of mist floating above the ponds, gray rags of cobweb caught in the bushes, ghostly gray toadstools circling the tree stumps. There is no sound but a sort of swishing of reeds in the dawn wind. Ssh! Did you hear something . . . a little drumming sound?

Tambourine

And isn't that tiny hoof-beats?

Plucked Strings

Oh, surely that is a Panpipe!

Piccolos

Quick! . . . Out of sight behind those bushes! This is what we came to see—the little fauns going to school. Yes, there is their teacher, an old satyr, leading them.

Now they are coming, marching two by two, the biggest ones first. . . . Oh, see those tiny fellows at the end! Pointed ears, little skipping goat-feet and funny scraps of tails! Did you ever in your life see anything so droll! Ssh . . . Don't frighten them . . . let them pass:

Muted Trumpets

Those shrill pipes will waken the whole woods. Don't you know the sleepy squirrels are grumbling, "There go those noisy school kids!" The fauns seem to be learning to march and to play the Panpipes at the same time.

I don't think much of their playing, do you? The old satyr isn't pleased with it either. Hear him urging them to try harder:

Oboe

They did try again, but they didn't change a single note. They only blew a little higher and shriller and made it sound worse.

See, they are making for that little hollow over there . . . it must be their classroom. Do you suppose the old satyr will have them practice scales? It might be a good idea.

Now they are almost out of sight . . . now . . . they are . . . gone! I wouldn't have missed that picture for anything, would you?

MARCH OF THE LITTLE LEAD SOLDIERS

If you were to listen to the army bands all up and down the land, you would not hear a more martial tune than this. It sounds exactly as a soldier's march should sound, brave and bright and businesslike. No missteps, no stooped shoulders, no tarnished buttons in this company, the music seems to say!

The music tells us something else about these soldiers. As our feet pick up the rhythm and we feel ourselves trying to march, we discover that we are several sizes too big. What short steps these fellows are taking! Surely they can't be real soldiers, not even children playing soldiers. They must be toy soldiers!

Why, it sounds almost like a toy band playing. Pierné has used only a few instruments, the wind instruments muted and the strings plucked to make them sound small and toylike.

First the trumpeter blows a bold flourish:

Echo answers. The drummer begins, "rub!—dub!—rub, dub, dub!"

The little feet mark time:

Then, "Forward, march!" The flute does its best to sound like a fife.

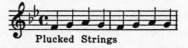

How stiff the tune is. But what would one expect for lead soldiers? The secret of its stiffness is in all those dots after the notes. Try taking the dots away and hear what happens to the soldiers!

Down below the tune we hear the little feet, marching, marching, in the strings:

Then the marching stops. The soldiers seem to be standing at attention. A pompous little tune steps forward:

It might be the toy general who has come out to review his troops. We just know they are saluting!

Oh, there is the trumpeter again. The troops mark time and march off. The sound of their band grows fainter. They must be leaving the parade ground, little lead soldiers turning into barracks:

Did anybody hear a box-lid close?

10.

Eduard Poldini

Budapest—1869

There are so many composers! Some of them, like Handel, Mozart, and Schubert, wrote all kinds of pieces, hundreds of them. Besides, they helped to make music's patterns and added new ideas which were useful to other composers. Because they gave most to music, they are called the great composers.

Then there were hundreds of others who wrote only a few pieces, perhaps only songs or short pieces for piano or violin, and were not interested in working out new kinds of music. Their music was often very good and gave pleasure to people of their own time. Some of it is still enjoyed. But because these men gave less to music, they are not rated as *great* composers, and little is known of their life stories. Fortunately this has nothing to do with their music or with our enjoyment of it.

We do not know much about the life of Eduard Poldini, but it cannot have been dull for notice how much of the map of Europe it has touched. He was born in Hungary. He had an Italian grandfather, from whom he got his Italian name. He went to school in Austria, France, and Germany. For a long time now, he has been living in Switzerland, in a beautiful place overlooking Lake Geneva. There are people who would add, "and from his music, you might think Poldini was a Frenchman."

Although he has written some light operas, Poldini is best known as a composer of piano music. He must be fond of fairy tales, for among his pieces we find such titles as *Snow White*, *The Gingerbread Witch*, and *Cinderella*.

THE DANCING DOLL

This is really a very famous little piece. Listeners of all ages love it. Some of the greatest pianists in the world have played it on their programs. The famous violinist, Fritz Kreisler, has borrowed it and arranged it for violin. Although it is a piano piece, it has even found its way into the orchestra!

There is a little introduction, to give the dancer the swing of the music. Then out she trips, the daintiest of French dolls, all curls and ribbons and stick-out skirts:

This tune surely calls for stiff little running steps and the whirls—you know, when the dancer lifts both arms like wings and twirls on her toes.

A new tune suggests a new step in the dance:

Now there is graceful bending and swaying. And there is such a pretty place where the long chord changes:

and lifts the whole tune up into a fresh new key:

Then the first tune tries to come back. But no, the swaying tune insists upon being heard again, and in a still higher key:

"Well," says the first tune, "if this is a climbing contest, I can climb too!" and up it goes for just a moment:

And so the two tunes play back and forth, and the pretty little doll dancer plays with them. Then, spreading his gauzy skirts in a trim curtsy:

she goes tripping off with not a curl out of place.

Did you notice how bright and clear-cut this music is, every line of it shining like a row of new pins? I suppose that is what the critics noticed about Poldini's music when they said it had a "jewel-like brilliance and polish."

The Dancing Doll always makes us wish we could hear more of Poldini's music. It may not be what musicians call great music, but it is good music which has pleased a great many listeners.

11.

Anatol Constantinovich Liadov

St. Petersburg—1855
Novgorod—1914

Anatol Liadov was the son of an orchestra conductor in an opera house in St. Petersburg, the old Russian city now called Leningrad. He was a sadly neglected little boy. His mother was dead and his father led a harum-scarum life, drinking and playing around with some of the frivolous theater people. Sometimes the father did not even see his two children for weeks at a time. He was so careless that often there was no food in the house, and the poor little boy and his sister had to borrow pennies from the servants to keep from starving.

Left to himself, Anatol spent a great deal of time playing at his father's theater. Everyone, from the leading singer to the lamplighter, made a pet of the little boy. He sometimes took part in the plays and operas, when crowds or processions were needed. He loved all this make-believe.

Anatol was not raised, he just grew. He had no idea of regular hours for eating and sleeping or of those habits of punctuality and order which make life pleasant. Of course he had no proper schooling. But he was a bright boy and very lovable. And he was so clever at music that someone took interest enough to send him to the conservatory.

Because rules meant nothing to him, Anatol was a troublesome schoolboy. His imp of mischief and his demon of laziness finally got him expelled from the conservatory. But one of his teachers saved him. This was Nikolai Rimsky-Korsakov, the man who composed *The Flight of the Bumblebee* and many other fine pieces. Young Anatol admired this great musician so much that he promised to do better, if only they would let him come back to his classes. To everyone's surprise the boy really worked. He had to use some queer methods, such as telling his sister, with whom he lived, not to give him any supper until he had finished his homework. But he kept not only the promise to behave, but also the promise of becoming one of the conservatory's most brilliant students. Rimsky-Korsakov spoke of him as "talented beyond telling."

After he graduated, Liadov taught for a while at the conservatory and also conducted the orchestra of the St. Petersburg Musical Society. He spent much of his time with that famous group of Russian composers known as "The Five." These men wanted Russian music to express Russian life and temperament, instead of sounding as if it might have been written in France or Germany. They used Russian folk music and Russian legends to give their music a true Russian feeling. Liadov helped them. His initials often appear in their work. But this likable fellow, who was so ready to help other people, was always quite indifferent about his own career. It grieved his friend Rimsky-Korsakov that Liadov, who might have done so much, did so little.

He wrote a number of charming pieces, many of them for the piano, which he played delightfully. His compositions were short and often left unfinished. It may have been his old demon of laziness still getting the better of him. Indifferent as he was, Liadov has been called "the wizard of Russian fairy tale and folk song."

DANCE OF THE MOSQUITO

When you can enjoy a mosquito in spite of his bad reputation, it really seems as if a wizard has been at work. Who could help enjoying Liadov's *Dance of the Mosquito?* Who would think of swatting this merry fellow?

First you hear that little warning *zzzz*, as if the tiniest of fairy aircraft were flying by. Muted violins make the sound, and this is how it looks when written:

Then comes the pleasant surprise! Instead of the needle prick and the red bump that usually follows such *zzzing,* you hear a jolly little dance:

Flute and piccolo caper on the thinnest of stilt-like legs, while the strings keep up a steady running up and down:

and the woodwinds make a contented, summery humming:

One of the funniest things about this dance is that while it is so very dainty, it is also a bit clumsy. For although the mosquito's legs are so cobwebby-fine that you can scarcely see or feel them when they alight on your skin, yet they are too long for graceful dancing. If you look closely at a picture of these legs, you'll find that some of them are bent at right angles. Maybe that explains the sharp-cornered feeling this dance has!

Don't miss the clever ending of the piece. The dancing is over, the *zzzing* begins again, just as at first, and we think we have seen the last of the mosquito:

But no, that *zzzing* takes on another tone! What does it mean? Is there to be another dancer? No, it is just the same fellow running back for his curtain call:

And there he goes, winging away!

This piece is sometimes called "The Dance of the Gnat," which is an equally good title since my dictionary says a mosquito is a kind of gnat. At the top of the score Liadov has told a secret in strange-looking Russian letters—"I have danced with the gnat." This music sounds as if he really has. Listening to it, we almost feel as if we too had danced with a mosquito.

The Music Box

A child of today may sit at home and hear a great orchestra play to him from a phonograph record, or he may tune in the radio and hear voices singing in far-off cities, or even across the ocean. It is a wonderful time to be alive!

But, strange as it may seem, the child of a hundred years ago thought that he too lived in the most wonderful time. Phonograph and radio had not yet been dreamed of, but he had a music box. What could be more marvelous than that?

There were all sorts of music boxes—big ones that sat on parlor tables, and tiny ones hidden in the most surprising places. Clocks, powder boxes, and snuff boxes were apt to play a tune at any moment. I have even seen a music box hidden in the bottom of a big mug. When you picked up the mug to drink, the thing began to play and kept right on with its tune until you set it down on the table! Music boxes were all the fashion in our great-grandfather's day.

Liadov's music box piece sounds exactly like one of those magic boxes of long ago. Liadov was very clever in choosing the instruments to play this piece. He chose a piccolo, flutes, and clarinets to play the tune because they can make such soft, clear, bell-like tones. Then he chose the harp and one of the chimes from the *glockenspiel*—the playing bells—to play the accompaniment.

This music box seems to have four tunes. This is the first:

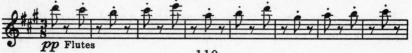

pp Flutes

Notice how sweet and tinkling it is, and how the harp keeps going back and forth on these few notes:

The second tune goes like this:

Then we hear the first one again, with some fancy little touches added by the clarinets.

Tune Number Three sounds more like an old-fashioned waltz tune:

In Number Four, the piccolo has a grand chance to show off its capers and bird trills:

Like most music boxes, this one plays its little tunes over and over until it runs down. But the pet tune is Number One. We hear it again and again. But it is so gentle, we do not grow tired of it. It is pleasant to picture some little boy or girl of long ago, listening, spellbound, to this wonderful new invention!

THE ENCHANTED LAKE

"Enchanted" is such a lovely word! Just hearing it seems to open a little window in the back of one's mind that lets in glimpses of wonderland. It is a pet word with children, so you may already know what it means. But did you ever try looking in the dictionary for a word you thought you knew well? It is a good way to get a surprise. The dictionary says that "enchant" means "to bewitch, charm or delight," which we already know. Then, in tiny type, at the very end, it says that it belongs to that family of words started by the old Latin word, *cantare*, meaning "to sing." Now this must mean that, in the beginning, "to enchant" meant to bewitch or charm with singing. It is a pretty idea for, after all, what is more enchanting than music?

"Enchanted" is scarcely the word to use for most of the lakes we know. It certainly does not fit America's five Great Lakes, so big and busy with winds and waves, and with boats and coal docks. Nor does it seem to suit the pleasure lakes, with their fringe of cottages and their putt-putting launches. But there are little lakes, usually up in the mountains or in the far North, that really do seemed charmed. In their forest frames they lie looking up at the sky, so blue and so quiet, just doing nothing! They scarcely seem to belong to a world of busy men, women, and children. Perhaps they have been enchanted by the music of nature—the bird choirs, the frog and cricket bands, and the sound of the wind in the trees!

It is just such a little spellbound lake that Liadov pictures in his music. Softly and slowly the instruments begin to speak in muted voices. The strings play a little wave-like figure:

Strings

The water ripples, but so slightly that it does not blur the picture of sky and clouds reflected in the lake's surface. Underneath, the cellos move back and forth in a gentle rockaby.

pp Cellos

From far above, come a few soft, staccato flute notes, like drowsy bird calls. Then, for just a moment, the music moves a little faster, as if the dreamers stirred in their sleep. A bird sings softly:

pp Flute

112

Somewhere, far down under the water, the sweet, sleepy voice of a nymph murmurs:

Then the bird notes fade into uncertain peeps. The water barely whispers. Even the little rippling breeze is caught in the spell, and the music dies away leaving the lake a shining, motionless mirror—enchanted water, enchanted birds, trees, clouds—enchanted listeners!

12.

Edward MacDowell

New York—1861
Peterboro—1908

Every American child should know about Edward Mac-Dowell. For he was an American boy who loved music and the out-of-doors, and he grew up to be America's first great composer.

Although Edward was a city child he had many chances to make friends with trees, flowers, birds, and animals. Sometimes his father would hitch up old Whitey, their horse, and take Edward and his brother off for a picnic in Central Park. Sometimes they would go to the river or down to the harbor to watch the big boats come in. And, best of all, sometimes they would go up to Grandfather MacDowell's farm and spend happy days in the real woods. Edward loved these days out-of-doors, and when it was time to go back to the city he would say, "I don't want to go home! I want to stay where the green fields and the trees are, and where the birds sing!"

But there were also nice things to do in the city. There were books. Edward loved his books—fairy tales, stories of knights, books about plants and animals, and books of travel and adventure. He liked pictures, too. He used to color the pictures in his books very carefully. Later he drew and painted pictures of his own. They were very good pictures for a child to have drawn. He also wrote fairy tales of his own and little verses about his friends the trees, the flowers, and the animals.

Soon after his eighth birthday, Edward began to have piano lessons. It was not long before his teacher, his mother, and even the neighbors knew that this little boy had a great musical gift. They liked to hear him play. They thought it quite unusual that a boy should love his music so much that he would sit at a piano for hours, making tunes of his own. He always could make music tell his stories and his dreams. He could even

114

make it paint little glimpses of the things he saw out-of-doors.

But Edward could do many other things besides making pictures, poems, and stories. He went to school with the other boys and was as full of mischief as anyone. He liked games and he liked fishing. They say he liked dancing, too. His quick eye and strong, steady hand made him good at all sorts of out-of-door sports. One time he even won a prize in a shooting match! Someone who knew him said, "He loved a fast and furious boxing match. The call of his soul won him for music and poetry. Otherwise he might have been a sea captain, a soldier, or an explorer in faraway countries. He had the fine body and he had the big manly spirit."

A wonderful thing happened to Edward when he was twelve years old. His mother took him to Europe. Edward and his mother had a glorious trip, and the boy came home determined to go back to Europe some day for a longer visit. The next three years Edward spent studying music. He had decided to become a professional piano player. When he was fifteen, Edward's family sent him to Europe again. This time he was to stay a long time and study. In those days we did not have such good schools and music teachers in the United States as we do today. Boys and girls could not learn their music comfortably at home, as you can.

Edward stayed in Europe for twelve years. Those were years full of hard work, for it takes a lot of hard work to make a real musician. But they were happy years. Edward loved his music better than anything in the world. He practiced and studied and later he gave lessons to other young students. Most interesting of all, he began to compose music. He had always made up little pieces, but hardly ever bothered to write them on paper, because he thought of himself as a piano player, not a composer.

One of his best pupils was a jolly American girl who, like Edward, had gone to Europe to study. She was interested in all of Edward's dreams and ideals and liked to hear him tell them in music. These two had such good times that they wanted to be together all the rest of their lives, and so they were married.

The MacDowells loved Europe and all that it had given them. But musicians from the United States began to beg them to come home and help make a musical America. So Edward

115

and Marian MacDowell brought their splendid gifts back to their own country.

For a while they lived in cities, teaching and playing concerts. But city crowds and noises always tired Edward MacDowell. He longed for the country. "The city," he once said, "is only a place in which to make money enough to get out into the country."

As soon as he could, MacDowell went to the country to live. He bought a deserted farm in the hills of New Hampshire. He made the old house bright and comfortable again and, because it stood on the top of a hill, he named it "Hillcrest."

The MacDowells loved their old farm. But its master had become so famous that even way off there in the country visitors came often. Sometimes they broke in upon the composer's precious dreams. So Mrs. MacDowell planned a lovely surprise for him. She knew a spot in the deep woods, near a spring, where MacDowell often walked with his dog. There he would sit under the pine trees, looking off over the lovely rolling country. There she had built a dear little, queer little, house. It is made of logs, with a bark door, and it stands on stilts so as to seem almost up in the treetops. It is just large enough to hold the things a composer would need for his day's work— his piano, his writing table, chairs, a cot on which to rest, and, of course, a few books and pictures. There is a fireplace made of cobblestones. On its cement hearth MacDowell himself scratched the names of these two good comrades—"Edward and Marian." Above the door he wrote:

A house of dreams untold,
It looks out over whispering treetops
And faces the setting sun.

It was truly a house of dreams. For here, with only the forest keeping him company, Edward MacDowell wrote much of his most beautiful music. It is music of the out-of-doors. I like to think that those forest sights and sounds have crept into the music. I fancy I can see and hear them as I listen.

When Edward MacDowell died, Mrs. MacDowell did a brave and beautiful thing. Instead of building a monument of stone to help people to remember her famous husband, she decided to honor his memory by making one of his dearest dreams come true. MacDowell had always helped other people.

116

When he was just a young fellow he had said, "The only thing in life is to be as useful as we can." When he found how much it helped him, and how happy it made him, to have his little house in the woods, he often said he wished other workers could have places like it. So Mrs. MacDowell wasted no time in thinking about how sad and lonely she was. She went to work giving concerts and saving all the money that came from MacDowell's music so that she might build other little houses in the woods on the New Hampshire farm. And every summer, poets, painters, and composers who are tired of city noises go up there and work out their dreams in the country quiet that MacDowell loved. They like to be where he has been and to see the place where he worked.

You could see the little "House of Dreams" if you went to Peterboro and drove out to "Hillcrest." And think of this, some day some one of you might make such good poetry or pictures or music that you would be invited to spend a summer in one of those forest workshops!

From Uncle Remus

All his life long, Edward MacDowell loved books. Two books which he read over and over again were *Uncle Remus, His Songs and His Sayings* and *Nights with Uncle Remus.* They are old plantation folk tales, retold by Joel Chandler Harris.

There are only two people in Mr. Harris' books—Uncle Remus, a dear old Negro, and Little Boy, who used to run away from the Big House to sit beside Uncle Remus' cabin fire and listen to the old man's stories.

And what stories they were! Now and then a two-legged creature called Mister Man is mentioned, but mostly the stories are about the exciting adventures of bears, foxes, possums, raccoons, rabbits, turtles, and other woodfolk. These animals are so real to Uncle Remus that he speaks of them as Br'er Wolf, Sis Cow, and Old Man Buzzard. But his favorite character is Br'er Rabbit.

We think of the rabbit as a scary little fellow, long in the ears and a bit short in the brain. But Uncle Remus makes him a hero. His Br'er Rabbit is full of mischief and gets himself and all the other creatures into the most awful scrapes. But though Br'er Bear is stronger, Mister Fox more cunning, and

117

Mr. Terrapin much wiser, it is always Br'er Rabbit who comes out on top!

Uncle Remus and Br'er Rabbit were among MacDowell's best storybook friends, so, of course, we find them in his music.

The piece called *From Uncle Remus* is different from most of the pieces we know. To discover its secret you have only to try to keep time to it. Imagine yourself marching to it. "I can't!" you say. "Just as I get in step, the tune runs away from me. This is no way for music to behave."

Now why do you suppose MacDowell used so many different tune patterns and such a mixture of fast and slow? Little Boy could have told you. Uncle Remus' stories went just that way! The important parts were slower, the exciting parts faster, and the voice went up and down, loud and soft, as voices always do when they are telling something interesting.

This piece is telling a story, so that is why it is different from the songs, the dances, and the marches we know. As you listen to it you may think it fits some particular Uncle Remus story. But I do not believe that Mr. MacDowell was trying to follow any one story. He meant this music to give the feeling of all the Uncle Remus stories. And from the music you can tell that they are merry stories, exciting in spots, but always with a happy ending.

There is no long "Once upon a time" to this story. Little Boy knew the characters too well to need it and, besides, he was always in such a hurry to hear what happened next!

The old man starts out rather slowly:

But right away things begin to happen:

and then:

From Uncle Remus copyright 1896, by P. L. Jung. Copyright renewed. Reprints by permission of The Arthur P. Schmidt Co., Inc.

and what do you think—of—that!

There is a second part to this story, you can tell exactly where it begins:

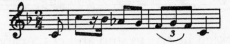

Toward the end, Uncle Remus comes back to the beginning, as if he were saying, "And so, you see, it was just as Sis Cow said in the first place—"

And notice the last notes, how gay they are. Why I almost think I hear the old man's chuckle:

and Little Boy's laugh:

Uncle Remus was a grand old storyteller. And Edward MacDowell was clever to make this storytelling tune.

OF BR'ER RABBIT

Br'er Rabbit has had his portrait made a good many times, for artists seem to like to paint this quaint little hero of Story Book Land. But none of his pictures is so lifelike as the one by his friend Edward MacDowell. It doesn't show his long ears, his powder-puff tail, or his furry coat. Music cannot paint that kind of picture. But how well it shows the funny little fellow who lives inside that furry coat, the real Br'er Rabbit.

We see Br'er Rabbit starting out on a fine summer morning:

Of Br'er Rabbit copyright 1902, by Arthur P. Schmidt. Copyright renewed. Reprints by permission of The Arthur P. Schmidt Co., Inc.

He is stepping along in the middle of the road, feeling as important as if he owned the whole world.

But no matter how dignified he tries to be, Br'er Rabbit can't be a really weighty fellow like the turtle, Mr. Terrapin. Impish thoughts just will go skittering through his fuzzy head:

and he is so tickled he has to stop and cut a caper, right then and there:

The more he thinks about his mischief, the bolder he gets. He begins to boast:

Then a sober thought creeps in among the gay ones. What if he were caught at his tricks? What if:

It wouldn't be at all funny if Br'er Fox really did get him and pop him into a cook pot! The jaunty little first tune droops its ears at the mournful thought:

But you can't keep a fellow like Br'er Rabbit down! Why should he be afraid, when he has the speediest legs in the woods?

His spirits rise:

and soon he is swaggering on his way again.

Things happen! There is no doubt about that. And from the way the music sounds, I should say it grew pretty exciting for a few moments. Then away goes Br'er Rabbit:

His little cotton tail is just a streak of white through the briar patch:

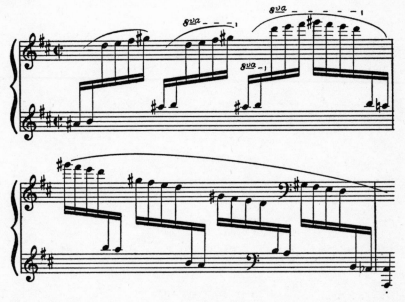

But as Uncle Remus used to say to Little Boy when Br'er got into a tight place, "Don't you worry 'bout Br'er Rabbit, honey. He ain't nebber been kotch *yit*, an' he ain't gwine ter be!" And

121

sure enough there he is, safe and saucy as ever:

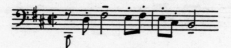

with a merry ha, ha:

for everybody who takes life too seriously!

They say that of all MacDowell's pieces, *Of Br'er Rabbit* was one of his greatest pets. He played it often and laughed a lot over it. I don't wonder that he liked it, do you?

5 6 7 8 9 10 11 12 13 14 15—BK—59